garden
ornaments

garden ornaments

A STYLISH GUIDE TO DECORATING YOUR GARDEN

Martha Baker
Photographs by Chuck Baker

Text with
Anne Marie Cloutier

CLARKSON POTTER/PUBLISHERS
NEW YORK

Copyright © 1999 by Martha Baker
Photographs © 1999 by Chuck Baker

All rights reserved. No part of this book may be
reproduced or transmitted in any form or by any means,
electronic or mechanical, including photocopying,
recording, or by any information storage and retrieval
system, without permission in writing from the
publisher.

Published by Clarkson N. Potter, Inc.,
201 East 50th Street, New York, New York 10022.
Member of the Crown Publishing Group.

Random House, Inc. New York, Toronto, London,
Sydney, Auckland
www.randomhouse.com

CLARKSON N. POTTER, POTTER, and colophon
are registered trademarks of Random House, Inc.

Printed in China

Design by Douglas Turshen
Illustrations by Susan Blubaugh
All black and white printing by Arista Labs, New York.

Library of Congress Cataloging-in-Publication Data
Baker, Martha.
Garden ornaments: a practical guide to decorating your
garden / by Martha Baker and Chuck Baker — 1st ed.
Includes index. (alk. paper)
1. Garden ornaments and furniture—United States.
2. Garden structures—United States.
3. Gardens—United States.
I. Baker, Chuck.   II. Title.
SB473.5.B34   1999
717'.0973—dc21   98-18876

ISBN 0-609-60264-0

10 9 8 7 6 5 4 3 2 1

First Edition

acknowledgments

GARDEN ORNAMENTS has been a journey with delightful moments at every turn in the road. It began long ago when Dabney Lancaster, dressed in a suit and his ever-present "bug fedora," introduced me to the joys of gardening. How can I ever forget my private golf cart ride through Westbury Gardens with ninety-two-year-old Peggy Phipps Boegner, who has lived her entire life on the estate. The near mystical experience of photographing Louise Humphries's Oriental garden in the fog on the Maine coast, and the creative rush of working with Bryan Antoni in his bizarre Miami retreat will always be remembered.

This journey would not have started without Deborah Geltman, whose determination and encouragement went well beyond the call of duty, and would not have continued without my husband, Chuck, whose magnificent photographs have brought my ideas to life.

Special thanks to my kids, Jesse, Emily, Charlie, and Hannah—their "input" was invaluable.

Along the road, Lisa Stamm and Dale Booher, John Barham and Dick Auer, Ellen Burnie, Susanne Lipschitz, Randy Carr, Michael Trapp, Bill Blass, Mac Hoak, and Libet Johnson were invaluable.

And last, special thanks to Annetta Hanna, John Son, Douglas Turshen, and Anne Marie Cloutier, who led us down the path.

MARTHA BAKER

contents

introduction

When I was nine years old, I dug up a patch of my mom's backyard to plant four-o'clocks, sweet peas, and zinnias—and I've been in love with the miracle of growing things ever since. Eventually, my pleasure in the planting, nurturing, and harvesting of gardens widened to include the creative satisfaction of designing them as well. It was a compelling subject that I was to study in earnest at college and as a postgraduate student and, later, to supplement through my travels in France, England, India, and other destinations nearer to home.

Over the years, I've developed a philosophy about garden design, which is that a garden should intimately reflect the lines and character of a home and, in fact, become an extension of it. The garden is an outdoor room whose components (plant materials as well as garden structures) should be handled in the same way as the corresponding decorative elements of an interior space—that is, to create a specific mood or style that is functional and aesthetically pleasing. Basically, that's what this book is meant to help you do. Here and in the following chapters, you'll learn how to choose from a variety of ornaments, such as paving, fencing, furniture, urns, pergolas, statuary, and fountains, and discover how to utilize them in ways that will best define and enhance your own personal vision of the ideal garden.

Admittedly, this "garden as room" idea didn't originate with us. Rather, it seems to have sprung from an innate, universal attitude about gardens that was evident as far back as the third millennium B.C. when the Egyptians, and other horticultural enthusiasts throughout the ancient world, began planting gardens within the walled enclosures surrounding their homes. Those enclosures—whether walls of stone or brick, or marble colonnades, or rows of trees or shrubs—had a special significance. Not only did they define the space within; in effect, they also laid claim to it. It was as if early civilized human beings were reserving for themselves one small share of the outdoors where, in an uncertain, often turbulent world, they could impose a sense of order and create an oasis of peace and beauty. When you think about it, that describes the goal of almost anyone who's ever planted a garden.

After establishing the perimeters of their outdoor space, old-world gardeners did what we today would instinctively do with any empty room—they furnished it with suitable materials. They laid down "flooring" and pathways that would be pleasant to walk on and look at. They planted flowers for pattern, color, and texture. They might have installed benches to rest upon, maybe an arbor for shade, and a pool or a fountain to cool the air and calm the spirit. For further interest and pleasure, they may have added statuary, urns, a bridge, or an ornamental arch—all placed with as much care and deliberation as they would have used when decorating the rooms in a house.

Throughout history, changing fashions in garden design have included the Middle Eastern pleasure garden, with its colorful tiles and plashing fountains; the small Japanese contemplative garden (especially popu-lar in cities where space is limited and the need for serenity especially acute); the lovely, grid-pathed monastery garden; the French parterre, as exemplified by the geometric formality of the gardens at Versailles and, in a smaller, more homespun version, at the Governor's Palace garden in Colonial Williamsburg; the neoclassical romantic garden, with its draping vines and "ruined" statuary; and the English estate garden, where landscape architects such as Capability Brown improved on nature by carving out huge vistas strewn with bridges, statuary, pavilions, and follies. To one degree or another, all of these styles have influenced contemporary garden design. In this book, you'll see variations of these and other classic examples, as well as garden styles unique to modern times. More importantly, you'll learn how to appreciate the basic elements of each in order to re-create whatever style you happen to favor.

Since my first backyard flower patch, not a summer has gone by without a garden of some sort in my life. I suppose my design philosophy was growing steadily with every garden I ever planned and planted. But the most exciting opportunity for putting it to the test was the seaside garden my family and I created for our getaway house in Shelter Island, New York.

The house itself, a three-story 1920s stucco, was a total wreck when my husband, Chuck, and I bought it in 1991. But, situated as it was right on the water, it seemed irresistible to our boat-loving family of two adults, four children, and a large dog. Realizing that it would take years to make all the improvements we had in mind, we made our top priority simply getting our new home into move-in shape. That done, we proceeded on the theory that something attractive was needed to distract the eye from our much-loved wreck

and vegetables and to add organic ingredients such as peat moss and fish emulsion to keep the plants fed and happy. But hardiness wasn't my only consideration. To me, plants are garden ornaments, too; they are to a garden what fabric, paintings, and other decorative elements are to a room. So, like the old-world gardeners I spoke of earlier, I selected plants in a range of textures, shapes, colors, and heights, a mix of delicate-looking blooms as well as bold, to create interest and contrast. Because everything that is added to a garden should contribute to the desired feel of it, I also included old-fashioned flowers, such as nasturtiums, heliotrope, and tea roses, to help establish the nostalgic mood I wanted to achieve.

Plant placement was another vital consideration. I didn't want the regimented effect that results from arranging short plants in the foreground and

tall plants behind. I wanted to surprise the viewer (including myself) with the unexpected. When you walk through our garden gate, the first thing you see is a row of giant hollyhocks whose long stems act as a frame for smaller plants peeking out from behind, such as purple salvia and coreopsis—or even the bright red globe of a ripe tomato.

As our seaside garden began to grow, so did the collection of ornaments chosen to enhance it. Collecting garden ornaments is a lot like choosing accessories for a living room. Sometimes you'll hunt for exactly the right piece to fill that empty space in the corner. Other times you'll just fall in love with a thing

of a house, so we got right to work on creating a garden.

I'd always wanted a seaside garden. What I had in mind was a French *potager,* or kitchen garden, with a comingled profusion of flowers and vegetables, plus a few ornamental touches of my own, seen against an ever-changing backdrop of sky and water. After clearing the site, laying the old-brick pathways, and installing a boundary fence, plant materials, and a variety of garden ornaments, my seaside garden finally became a reality that now looks as colonial and countrified as I first envisioned it.

At the beginning of the project, people told me I'd never be able to grow anything so close to the water. But somehow, despite the salt air, occasional flooding by seawater and storms, and other adverse conditions —or possibly because of them—the garden positively thrives. One reason for its success is the plants themselves. I was careful to select hardy types of flowers

and decide to buy it first and figure out what to do with it later. Such was the case when the kids and I were scouring a London antiques shop and came across three disk-shaped wire forms. They were about three feet in diameter and looked a little like squashed spirals. I have no idea what they were used for originally, and at the time I had even less of a clue about how we'd use them. But despite that small drawback (as well as Chuck's initial skepticism), we carted them all back home with us. Eventually we turned them into topiaries by hoisting them up on seven-foot lengths of metal pipe (courtesy of the town dump) and covering the tops with silver-lace vine. Now these umbrella-like structures stand along our seawall next to the garden like northern versions of the *palapas* that dot tropical beaches. The bonus, and also the original intent, is that they provide us with shade without blocking our view of the water.

The garden has additional topiary in the form of a fence, which we had specially made for the purpose, as is occasionally necessary when a certain type of garden structure is needed. Originally, we'd put up a Nantucket-style picket fence, but when the town fathers objected, we devised an alternative that did get official approval: a green grid of sturdy lobster wire fashioned to mimic the curved top of the age-mellowed brickwork forming the opposite garden wall. Today, the grid is all but hidden beneath a lush blanket of flowers and vines. Aside from keeping out four-legged pests, and adding the needed architectural element of a vertical line, the fence also establishes the garden's scale (something to keep in mind when you're working within a large amount of acreage, as we were). As I see it, for a garden to feel like a room, it should be room-sized and enclosed by boundaries such as a fence, a wall, or a hedge.

Many ornaments in our garden come from the big outdoor antiques shows held every year in Brimfield, Massachusetts. Dealers and other intrepid collectors show up in the middle of the night with flashlights to see their way through the goods. This is just part of the fun for us—along with figuring out how to fit all our purchases into the Suburban. One of our biggest challenges was a ten-foot-high and enormously heavy obelisk-shaped cast-iron piece, whose original purpose was a mystery. It ended up in the garden because it's an interesting object on which to grow roses.

This leads us to another point about garden ornaments: the necessity for choosing interesting-looking objects that stir the senses and stimulate the imagination. It doesn't matter whether you bought the piece at Sotheby's or found it lying around somewhere. In fact, we discovered a stone bench in three separate pieces lying half buried on our property. Now it sits snugly

against the garden wall looking weathered and ancient, which is just what makes it so interesting.

It's important to arrange garden ornaments in interesting ways. The whole point of a garden is to move the viewer from point A to point B in a kind of narrative that changes, surprises, and pleases at every turn. As you walk through a garden, something may cause you to pause—maybe an urn placed in the middle of a walkway, or an ornamental pond—so that you have to walk around it or continue down another path. Or the level of the ground changes, so that you suddenly have an overview into an outdoor space lying below you. A visitor once described our garden as having "something interesting to look at wherever you turn." I thought that it was one of the loveliest compliments a gardener could receive.

A more recent improvement on our property is a brick-paved courtyard garden, where I grow herbs and flowers in a variety of pots and urns. Unlike the seaside garden, this spot lies protected from maritime winds within two embracing walls of the house, with the other two sides enclosed by shrubs, flowers, and vines. The house—still a work in progress but greatly improved—has been restuccoed and painted a creamy yellow-pink to resemble the old, soft-hued cottages in the French countryside. Low wooden boxes painted a deep black-green drip with tendrils of ivy at every window, and a spiral-shaped topiary or two further arrest the eye.

As you've probably gathered by now, my view of the perfect garden is a very personal one—as it should be. Every garden should express the unique character and tastes of its owner. With this in mind, Chuck and I wanted *Garden Ornaments* to be a practical guide as well as an inspirational source, both for experienced gardeners and for nongardening readers interested in creating (or having a professional create) unique garden rooms of their own. Each chapter is devoted to several versions of a single style, ranging from the romantic to the urban with numerous types in between. We've also made a point of focusing on the individual elements in each garden that contribute to its special look.

On these introductory pages, you see photographs of our garden spaces as they are. Later you'll see this and other settings transformed to show the many different effects that can be achieved by the clever use of key garden furnishings and ornaments. These are pieces you'll be able to find in stores and catalogs listed in the detailed Resource Guide at the end of the book. The guide contains invaluable sources for common and hard-to-find garden ornaments and furniture, whether new or old. There's a listing of antiques shops and annual antiques shows as well. Finally, we've also included step-by-step how-tos for "weathering" new pieces and for making some of your own garden ornaments from scratch.

While traveling through the United States and elsewhere to compile the photographs and information for this book, Chuck and I visited a number of beautiful gardens and met with the delightful people who own them. The whole process was a hectic, often exhausting, but thoroughly gratifying experience for both of us, and now that it's done, we hope you'll be as pleased with the result as we are.

the classical garden

UNTIL FAIRLY RECENTLY, most formal gardens were designed in the classical style or were influenced, to a greater or lesser degree, by classical elements. But when asked point-blank, "What is a classical garden?" I often hesitate in giving an answer. The basic elements, of course, involve a formalized arrangement of plant materials and the symmetrical placement of ornaments such as statues, pergolas, trellises, pools, fountains, and benches. The garden style is, well, *ordered.* But this bare-bones answer never seems adequate.

For one thing, a classical garden is so much more than the sum and arrangement of its parts. There's a psychological component to it that can be instinctively sensed but is hard to express in words. There's also the problem of accumulated influences on the basic style: Like every great idea that has ever gained popularity, classical style has been added to and subtly reshaped by innumerable cultures over centuries. In eighteenth-century English garden design, for example, the use of architectural surprises—such as Chinese pagodas and classic temples—was a romantic rebellion against classicism; today, these elements are considered part of it. As a result, it's possible to ask three different peo-ple to describe a classical garden and get three completely different answers—all of them right.

In order to appreciate the definitive character of a classical garden, we have to return to its origins and recapture the worldview of the people who created it. Whenever Western scholars use the word *classical* in the historical sense, they're referring to works of art produced by the Greeks during their Golden Age in the fifth century B.C. This was an intensely creative era driven by the humanistic beliefs of the times. In Greek philosophy and art, the human form was admired and idealized. The human order was considered to be in harmony with the natural order, which, in turn, was held to have been created for human happiness. The catchwords of the day were "restraint," "balance," "order," and "symmetry" (and pretty valid concepts they were, too, when you consider what they produced in the visual arts alone—including the art of garden design).

In ancient Greece, houses often featured beautiful walled courts or gardens bordered by a colonnade. In Rome, which welcomed the Greek tradition and became identified with classicism by spreading that tradition throughout the Western world, the wealthy built lavish terraced gardens featuring sculpture, porticoes, and banquet halls.

Sculpture, an essential element of the classical ideal, consisted of exquisite, lifelike renderings of the human body at its most perfect. Flowers and plants were not used as they grow in nature but were arranged and balanced by size, color, and shape. Water was not allowed to flow naturally but was captured and controlled within a pleasing geometric boundary. Furniture was chosen not just for comfort's sake but also for ornament and was designed with the same restrained simplicity that characterizes a Greek temple. Trellises, pergolas, obelisks, and urns were chosen and carefully placed to achieve both a sense of harmony and of unity within the whole.

For two millennia, the classical style has been adopted and adapted; the Mediterraneans modified it, the English softened it, the French fine-tuned it with unparalleled, slide-rule precision. In western Europe and America, it has been admired, copied, rejected, then rediscovered and infinitely redefined.

But even with all these changes, the truly classical garden still retains a unique psychological essence. When you encounter such a garden, you

invariably experience relaxation and contentment. The reason for this lies in those deceptively simple concepts of restraint, balance, order, and symmetry—the ideals that shaped our Western cultural tradition. And tradition, the instant recognition of the familiar with its reassurance of continuity, is what the classical is about. Classical style offers a reminder of the ideals by which our standards were set, and this, finally, is the essence of a classical garden and the source of its comfort—just as it has been since the beginning.

great american classic

Even in rural Dutchess County in New York State, an area known for its scenic beauty, this classical garden is not only a standout but also one of the increasingly rare "great" gardens in America. Located within a large private estate, it features formal plantings surrounded by a stunning curved trellis that is painted in the same shade of blue found at Hidcote, one of England's great gardens in the Cotswolds. That trellis—with its suggestion of Greek column, Roman arch, French-inspired lattice, and English-imported Chinese pagoda—is a good example of the accumulated influences on classical.

Another impressive element is the owner's use of statuary. It includes classical antiques as well as a spectacular modern sculpture of children running hand in hand that is a spiritual descendant of classicism in its idealistic vision and realistic execution. The impact of each statue's placement—at the end of a walkway, in a niche by a pool, in the foreground of a parklike landscape—isn't just visual, it's visceral. With the delightful surprise of discovery comes an inner reactive "yes!" at the rightness of a statue being exactly there, or here, in that spot or this.

ABOVE, LEFT A garden shed with classic lines inspired by a Chinese pagoda. LEFT A slatted wood planter like this is perfectly scaled for topping a narrow wall. OPPOSITE A statue used as a focal point for a pergola-covered walk.

ABOVE A panoramic view of the lovely sunken garden surrounded by the eclectically classic style of the trellis. The female figure in the foreground is the same one shown facing the pergola walk on the previous page, but from this perspective, it's seen as a focal point for the entire garden. When statues are centrally placed in this way, it's especially important that their detailing is nicely carved and interesting to look at, no matter what the viewing angle. ABOVE, RIGHT Another beautifully rendered piece is this female nude with a clinging cherub that seems to rise up from the center of a flower bed. The tree in the background becomes just that—a dark ground for the light-colored stone so that the statue stands out even more vividly from its surroundings. BELOW, NEAR RIGHT One key element within the classic tradition is symmetry—that is, the correspondence in size, form, and arrangement of pieces on opposite sides of a given point. A nice demonstration of that concept is this pair of antique stone urns positioned on either side of a wall-bordered walk. FAR RIGHT An antique stone planter richly designed with a bas relief of child figures and swags of fruit. Elongated pieces like this one are excellent for establishing all (or part) of a garden boundary wall.

a garden in winter

Early in this project, Chuck and I decided we wanted to photograph a garden as it looks in winter—and this is the one we had in mind. Seeing it reminded us of our two years in France where we used to visit Loire Valley châteaux with their lovely formal gardens. Here was the same symmetry of arrangement, the same aura of antiquity and restraint, that has typified French classical gardens since Le Nôtre began creating them for Louis XIV.

Located in a swath of wooded hills that cuts through the southeast corner of New York State, the property belongs to Stephen Sills and James Huniford. The talent they bring to their highly successful Manhattan interior-design business, Sills Huniford Associates, is evident in their garden.

Because the land has a number of level changes, the owners erected low stone walls to define a series of terraced rooms, and within these spaces, the French influence is everywhere: in the precisely clipped boxwood spheres set on a patio like chess pieces on a board; in the geometric pattern of the driveway; and especially in the impressively arranged antique ornaments—balls, urns, columns, and obelisks. For much of the year, the contours of these ornaments are softened by plants, but in January shapes and details are laid bare by the winter light—just as we had imagined it.

OPPOSITE A stairway connecting two terraces. ABOVE, RIGHT Re-creation of a 17th-century parterre. RIGHT A collage of antique architectural fragments.

LEFT Typical of the antique
embellishments in this garden is a
lichen-encrusted, 18th-century
Italian urn with a gargoyle bas relief.
OPPOSITE Running alongside
one of the stone boundary walls is
a lovely carpet-design drive
composed of concrete grid pavers
filled in with manicured grass.

ABOVE, RIGHT The cement shapes
include a three-dimensional Belgian
star that's thought to be a charm
against evil garden spirits. ABOVE In
a courtyard paved with bluestone,
meticulously sculpted spheres of
English boxwood sit in their own gravel
beds like chess pieces on a board.
RIGHT An impressive boundary wall is
established by a stately colonnade
of towering limestone pillars topped
with neo-classic bronze urns.

LEFT Symmetry is a requisite in the classic tradition and this garden honors that concept down to the smallest details. For example, on the stairways connecting the property's multilevel terraces, the stone wall columns on each side are capped with matching cement finials like the one focused on here. The encircling vines, which also adorn the stone risers, columns, and walls, are another way of establishing the garden's unmistakable air of *ancien régime.* BELOW, LEFT and BELOW Two views of the formal French gravel court that skirts the drive. The enclosure pedestals and the corner obelisk are all limestone architectural pieces recovered from an 18th-century castle outside Paris.

the garden at virginia house

Virginia House, in Richmond, Virginia, wasn't named for the state, as you might suppose, but rather for the much-loved wife of retired ambassador Alexander Woodell, who had the house built in the 1920s, incorporating stones from a ruined seventeenth-century English priory. When landscape architect Charles Gillette was commissioned to design a classical garden for the house, his plans included an intimate, feminine retreat, known familiarly as "Madam's Garden," which features a small ornamental pool and a striking clay figure of a discus thrower poised in midaction above it.

We know that Gillette was a great admirer of the English architectural visionaries Lancelot "Capability" Brown and Sir Edwin Landseer Lutyens. Their influence on classical garden design can be seen in the variety of statues, benches, and urns that ornament the property, and in the terraced gardens (an idea the English borrowed from the Mediterraneans) that overlook the lovely Virginia countryside.

But as you saunter from space to space, you find still another classical influence—the creative use of brickwork (a Roman legacy) in garden structures and stairways, in herringboned paving, in open-worked balustrades, and in walls framing a classical bas-relief or a decorative cement filigree.

Some statues are regarded as "keepers of the garden." Here, that role is served by a tubby, turbaned sentry that adds a delightful touch of whimsy to an otherwise classical setting.

PREVIOUS PAGE Low walls of stone and brick delineate the lovely landscaped terraces that were built to accommodate the sloping land and take full advantage of the rolling countryside view. OPPOSITE An antique urn nestled into the plant growth atop a stone column. ABOVE Set into a garden wall, a bas relief dramatically framed by tendrils of ivy. LEFT A gracefully styled bench of stone positioned in front of the niche of an arching brick wall. BELOW, LEFT Another of the garden's guardians is this amusing piece of statuary that looks like a classical parody of the Sun King, Louis XIV. BELOW The pussycat's perch is a curved stone bench with unusual animal carvings for legs. Behind it, the openwork brick wall mimics the concave shape of the bench placed before it.

a classic
in miniature

Large estates and historic houses aren't the only places where classical gardens are found. They're equally at home on smaller properties such as this pretty East Hampton, New York, residence belonging to Charlotte Moss. Most of the wonderful objects that grace her garden are easily found reproductions, proving that classical ornaments don't have to be antique to be effective.

An interior decorator by profession, Moss has put her personal stamp on the classical style by choosing plant materials in predominant shades of maroon and chartreuse (her favorite color scheme) and by arranging ornaments in arresting vignettes that evoke a sense of civilized domesticity in the garden.

When ornaments are fashioned after classical models, they tend to look antique, even when they're not—as is the case with this column-mounted armillary presiding over a lush little flower bed on the lawn.

Greens spilling gracefully over
the front of a stone planter;
a wheeled container for garden
refuse offers a handsome
solution for a practical need;
finials lined up along a stone
wall; a quality reproduction of a
"ruined" Greek statue setting
the classical theme for the
entire garden. OPPOSITE A wide
wooden chaise finds a perfect
niche in the garden wall.

sculpture
showcases

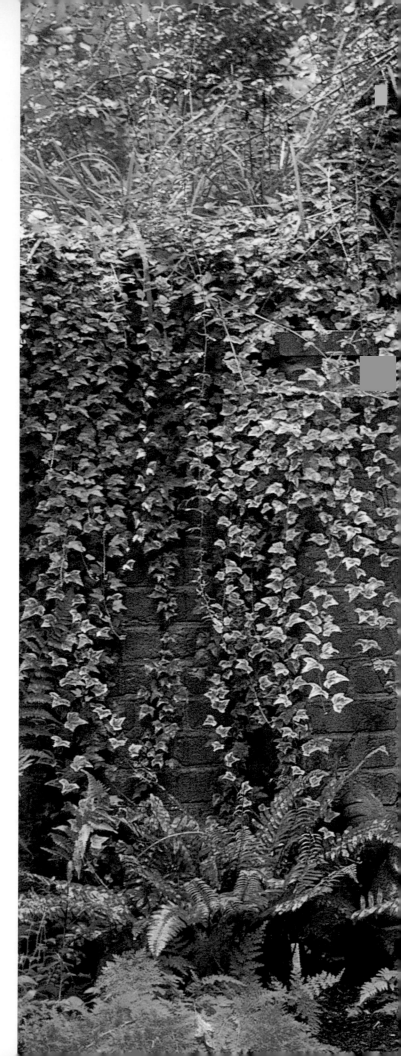

Carrington Brown is a talented land-scape designer who has helped create some of Richmond, Virginia's, most beautiful gardens. The ornaments she chose for the classical gardens shown here are a mix of antiques, faithful reproductions of antiques, and the unique work of local artisans. Whatever the source, each piece—such as the exquisite female nude figure set in a rose garden—is distinctly classical in feeling.

Sometimes clients commission Brown to design a showcase for pieces they already own, as did a woman who inherited a valuable bronze statue of a laughing child holding two turtles, an original work by sculptor Edith Barretto Parsons. The result was an enchanting garden space with parquet-patterned brick paving, classically rendered armchairs, and a leafy niche that perfectly frames the charming little figure rising from a fountain pool.

A fireplace is a good example of
how traditional indoor comforts can be
translated to the outdoors. This
one—complete with chimney, mantel,
and vines—positively invites the
drawing up of chairs, the telling of tales.

OPPOSITE The bronze Parsons sculpture of a laughing boy with turtles is an important piece originally purchased by the owner's mother. Now residing in its own leafy bower above a fountain pool, it's the dominant feature of a small brick-paved garden patio. ABOVE In another Virginia garden—an elegant little figure that's the essence of youthful femininity. Though the piece is a reproduction, its classic subject and fine detailing establish an aura of antiquity.

personalized classic

When John Barham and Dick Auer retired from the world of business, they exchanged one full-time occupation for another: collecting ornaments for their garden. Located in Bridgehampton, New York, on what was once a potato field, the serene expanse of grass, trees, and flowers is adjacent to a Southern-style Georgian house built for them by a Virginia architect in the early 1990s. The classical lines of the house are perfectly complemented by the garden pieces that surround it. The eclectic mix includes magnificent animal sculptures, a curved pathway of giant millstones, a vine-covered arbor dripping with wind chimes, and an impressive collection of antique birdhouses on high poles that line the garden like friendly sentinels. This garden combines traditional and nontraditional elements to express the feeling of classicism in a uniquely personal way.

The pool's entrance gates and fencing
are compelling examples of Georgian
design reduced to its essence. And
leading the way to them is a walkway
made of giant millstones which
the owners spent years collecting.

While animal subjects were of secondary importance in early Greece's artistic lexicon, they still held a place within the classic ideal. In this garden, we see a very individual view of that ideal, where lavish landscaping provides a perfect home for the owners' eclectic menagerie of animal statues, as well as for other collected pieces.

ABOVE A sweet-faced monkey peeks out at passersby from behind some greenery. LEFT A startlingly lifelike (if oversized) praying mantis sculpture. BELOW, LEFT A matched set of horse-head hitching posts positioned on each side of a garden path. BELOW, RIGHT A collection of breeze-catching wind chimes swing from the branches of an arbor roof. OPPOSITE Among the most impressive of the garden denizens is the delicately rendered antelope on a stone plinth.

MAKING AN OBELISK

In ancient Egypt, the obelisk was associated with sun worship, which, no doubt, explains why it's always seemed so at home in a garden setting. Whether it's supporting plants or standing alone, this classic ornament works with many design styles, and is comparatively easy to make yourself.

BEFORE YOU START, read through all the directions. Also see page 200 for general wood-project guidelines.

FOR THIS PROJECT YOU'LL NEED:

- Four 6-foot-long two-by-twos (for the legs) and three 8-foot-long one-by-twos (for the horizontal pieces) of either redwood or cedar
- A crowning ball finial, 2½ to 3 inches in diameter (available in lumberyards or home-project stores)
- Galvanized flat wood screws, 1½ and 2½ inches long
- A tape measure and pencil
- A wood saw
- An electric drill

STEP 1: From the three 8-foot one-by-twos, cut four each of the following lengths for the horizontal pieces: 20 inches, 17 inches, 14 inches, 12 inches, and 7 inches.

STEP 2: Lay two of the 6-foot two-by-twos on the ground to form an isosceles triangle whose legs are 16 inches apart at the

triangle's base. Use a 2½-inch screw to connect the two legs together about an inch below where they touch at the top. Because the pieces meet at an angle, the screw will show between the pieces, but this will be covered by the obelisk's finishing "crown" of molding.

STEP 3: Lay one of the 20-inch pieces across the triangle (wide side up) so that its bottom edge measures 12 inches from the bottom of each triangle leg and extends out at least ³/₄ inch beyond each side; these extensions will be sawed off later. Using 1½-inch screws, attach the piece to each leg.

STEP 4: Position and attach one each of the 17-inch, 14-inch, and 12-inch pieces, in that order, as described in Step 3, so that the bottom edge of each piece is 12 inches above the piece below it and extends at least ³/₄ inch beyond each side.

STEP 5: Position and attach the 7-inch piece at the top of the triangle so that its top edge just hides the top outer angles of the two legs.

STEP 6: Repeat Steps 2 through 5 to make the second side of the obelisk.

STEP 7: Saw off the projecting ends of all the horizontal pieces on both of the triangles you just assembled so that the trimmed edges follow the angle of (and are flush with) the legs.

STEP 8: Set the two triangular sides upright so that the tops are leaning against each other and there's a 16-inch space between the two triangles at the bottom. Use two 2½-inch screws to attach the two triangles to each other at the top.

STEP 9: With the obelisk still in an upright position, follow Steps 3 through 5 to attach the remaining horizontal pieces to the two open sides of the obelisk. Saw off all the projecting ends so that they follow the angle of (and are flush with) the sawed ends of the horizontal pieces on the first two triangles you assembled.

STEP 10: Attach the finial to the top of the obelisk, and stain or paint the structure as desired.

CLASSICAL ELEMENTS

You don't have to live on an impressive estate to own a classical garden. If the furnishings you choose are traditional in feeling, they'll establish the classical theme all by themselves. And that holds true whether you're choosing one-of-a-kind antiques or more affordable reproductions.

Before there were clocks and watches, there were sundials in the garden. This unusual example features a stone square on a pedestal that was copied from an antique model.

A wooden garden bench has beautifully balanced lines that immediately declare it a classic. Another indication is the Grecian-white paint finish, a traditional color in classic design.

Valuable antique models of classic stone garden urns have always been prized by those who are able to afford them. For those who can't, the next best thing is a faithful reproduction like this one.

An obelisk is another garden tradition. The familiar elongated shape not only helps to establish a classic theme, it also adds a pleasing vertical to balance the horizontals around it.

Shown amid the classical ruins are wonderful reproductions of classic English garden furniture that include a teak dining table, matching chairs, and a canvas and teak sun umbrella large enough to shade a whole patio.

While pairs of antique stone lions are often used to adorn the side columns of estate entrances, they're also found in classical gardens. This beautifully carved beast is in an estate garden in New York.

the waterside garden

I USED TO WONDER why people were so insistent about having a house on the water—until we moved into one ourselves. Then I understood the heady feeling that comes with "owning" the horizon, as if the water and sky were an extension of my land and belonged to me. When a garden is situated on such a site, it's like having a room with a view—one whose mood constantly changes with the passing hours, the fluctuating weather, the progressing seasons. On some days the water may be fog-softened and mysterious; on others, all sun-glittered and bright. Even the dark, wave-tossed broodiness of an approaching storm has its own kind of beauty. So when choosing ornaments for a lakefront or a seaside garden, you'll want to keep in mind the visual impact of your unique backdrop.

The most important thing is to capture or frame the view wherever you can and avoid blocking it. Think in terms of open, airy structures that let you see glimpses of the water through them. If you want to define your garden area, for example, avoid a solid wall. Instead, opt for an open-worked metal fence or a wooden one with water-framing spaces between the slats. Better yet, you might want to skip fencing altogether and establish your perimeters unobtrusively with ground-hugging plants, a series of rocks, or a few small stone sculptures strategically placed at the boundary corners.

Another terrific way to make the most of the vista is by introducing an ornamental arched gate that looks out on it. I've found that kind of structure invariably draws you toward it to see the view that it frames.

From a more practical standpoint, an exposed waterfront garden needs some provision for shade. A pergola, such as the one that is shown on page 51—is ideal. To build it, we topped four tall columns with a rectangular frame to receive a roof of snow fencing. Then we planted vines around the perimeter. From this shady space we can enjoy the view as sunlight filters down through the tracery of vines and slivers through the open columns that support them.

The pergola brings up a key point about a seaside garden, which has to do with line and balance. The horizon line is always present, so you'll need to add a few vertical elements to balance out the strong horizontal. Does this mean you should avoid horizontals? Not at all. In fact, the pergola roof itself is one, but it is countered by vertical support columns. The same balancing principle holds true for structures such as tables, for example. Because a waterfront garden is such a wonderful place for entertaining, I love having a large table there on which to work, prepare food, and dine. Chairs arranged around the table automatically introduce vertical elements that counter the horizontal of the table surface.

Dining chairs may come and go as needed, but you'll want to install more permanent kinds of seating for occasions when you invite friends for a drink or to just settle in for a good chat. This might be a pair of slatted lounge chairs, with a small table between them for glasses and such, that are carefully positioned to enjoy the sunset. You'll want to include a stone bench or two—not only for sitting, but also because the simple, elegant lines of such pieces can be striking against the open space behind them.

It goes without saying that all garden ornaments should be weather resistant, but that's doubly important for a waterfront garden, which has much more weather to contend with. Look for materials that can withstand corrosive salt air (if you live by the sea) and constant dampness—these include rustproof metals, decay-resistant woods, and natural stone—and

that are sturdy enough to stay put in high winds. You don't want anything that's going to blow away onto your neighbor's property or end up as so much flotsam on the beach. That's why canvas umbrellas or awnings might not be good choices: unless specially treated, canvas will mildew after a time, and sunshades are usually too light to remain stationary on very windy days.

I've always been partial to using rough-hewn, natural materials in a waterfront garden, the kind you're likely to find in the environment itself or that can easily adapt to it. These might include primitive sculptures that look as if they grew out of cliff rock, walkways carpeted with beach pebbles or patterned with brick (the clay for which often comes from the seabed), or maybe a cement urn or a birdbath encrusted with seashells.

There are other ways to make use of this unique environment as well. For instance, you could hang some wind chimes to echo the sounds of buoys and ships' bells. A flagpole would also fit in perfectly; our seaside garden has one that Chuck whittled down from the trunk of a dead pine tree. I love listening to the halyard snap in the wind and seeing how the flag billows out from it—a delight to the eye as well as the ear.

oriental style

As you travel along the seacoast of Maine, you find a recurring garden theme that seems to marry the wild beauty of the rocky, forested shore with the classic elements of Japanese and Chinese decorative styles. This garden is one of the best examples of that happy union.

Begun in the 1930s, when the Asian influence on Western outdoor ornament was at its height, the garden evolved as successive generations of the same family traveled throughout the Far East and brought back gates, pagodas, statuary, and other ornamental pieces associated with its ancient cultures. When we came upon the garden, it and the island-dotted seascape were shrouded in a typical Maine coast fog. Seeing those distinctive Asian structures emerging from the mist evoked such feelings of mystery and timelessness that we decided to photograph the garden for this book exactly as we had seen it then.

A dramatic ornamental gate, featuring cutout wooden doors and two dragons winging out from the lintel roof, makes a striking silhouette against the fog-shrouded coastal view.

ABOVE Its contours blurred by
the passage of time and weather, the
small figure of a Buddha sits in
peaceful repose within a rocky niche.
ABOVE, RIGHT One of the garden's
many antiques is this exquisite
carved-wood miniature of a teahouse.
RIGHT A fox on a log, carved from an
actual log, is typical of animal
sculptures found in Chinese gardens.
BELOW A lichen-covered stone wall
reinforces the sense of serene
antiquity. OPPOSITE A six-sided stone
lantern, an ornamental piece so
indigenous to oriental gardens, looks
equally at home in this rocky coastal
garden in Maine.

a coastal woodland garden

Farther along the Maine coast, sculptor Katie Bell's cliffside dwelling looks out over the seemingly untamed expanse of rocks and trees bordering beautiful Seal Harbor. It was this primitive setting that during the 1930s inspired a Harvard-based group of settlers in the area to build a number of so-called "rusticator cottages" such as hers. The seaside garden that Bell created for herself seems to take up this theme of earthy munificence as naturally as if it came ready-made from some ancient civilization.

Walking over the property, you discover rolling carpets of moss and little sun-filtered glades where Bell has placed selected pieces of her own voluptuous, organic-looking sculpture as well as other works in stone. In such a rugged setting, with its natural woodlands and outcroppings of rock, the pieces look as if they've been carved out of—or grew out of—the very landscape surrounding them.

ABOVE, LEFT A sensual female torso rises from a wild garden bed. LEFT A limestone abstract of a mother and child. From a purely visual standpoint, it's an interestingly shaped mass that nicely fills the open space within a thicket of pines. OPPOSITE Two ocean-liner deck chairs on the back porch look out on a becalmed Seal Harbor.

Katie Bell is a professional sculptor whose stone figures are characterized by their primitive sensuality. So where better to display them than in the equally primitive setting of her coastal woodland garden? Whether placed in a leaf-strewn clearing or perched on a trellis wall, each piece has the organic look of having been chiseled from a standing rock that's been there since the Creation. ABOVE The reclining female figure, entitled *Minoan Dream*, wasn't carved from standing stone but from a large block of sandstone that was once used for ballast in an old ship. The block was recovered from the wreckage after the ship foundered on Little Cranberry Island not far from Bell's Seal Harbor garden. ABOVE, RIGHT The flat top of a garden trellis wall makes a good spot for showing off smaller ornamental pieces—like this wonderful, flat-featured head that Bell sculpted from Belgian black marble.

NEAR RIGHT When this crowned king's head of pink Georgian marble accidentally broke, Bell just propped the pieces back together in her garden where they now assume the aspect of an Indian totem. FAR RIGHT A heart-stone sculpture reposes on a picturesque tree stump.

seaside nostalgia

For Edie Landecke, a medical doctor with a demanding New York City practice, gardening is a form of relaxation therapy. Visiting her seaside garden in Shelter Island, New York, makes it easy to understand why. Hers is a rose-covered-cottage getaway that's serene and intimate in feeling. There are wonderful nostalgic ornaments, such as an old shell-covered birdbath fountain, nestled among the flowers and plants she tends assiduously. Overlooking the water is a sweep of velvety lawn. Because of the property's unique location, it's possible to watch the sun going down and the moon coming up without stirring from the Edwardian settee. Considering how restful it all is, there's not much incentive for wanting to do that anyway.

OPPOSITE Setting the mood is a vintage settee whose white cast-iron tracery suggests the old-fashioned crochet work that once adorned mantel fringes and antimacassars. ABOVE, RIGHT The charming bird-in-a-birdbath fountain recalls an earlier, gentler age. It's one of four such pieces on the island, made by the same artisan using beach pebbles from local shorelines. RIGHT A cozy retreat with all the components of a classic storybook cottage by the sea.

a collector's retreat

Sea views combined with coastal woodlands make a particularly dramatic backdrop for sculptural art in this secluded island garden in Maine. The owners, who are serious collectors of sculpture, commissioned Ron Cross to create an abstract piece in cast iron called *The Wave.* It deserves the prominent place it holds on one of the grassy plateaus flanking a flower-filled garden. The garden, which overlooks the sea, is enclosed by a beautiful curved retaining wall of local stone that's a sculptural ornament in itself.

ABOVE, LEFT In this seaside retreat, even functional pieces look like sculptural art. A good case in point is this aerodynamic canvas awning positioned over a sunny porch. LEFT Between the house and the sea a retaining wall built with local stone holds back a spectacular flower border. OPPOSITE The garden's main focal point is a fabulous cast-iron sculpture by Ron Cross which captures the movement of tossing waves.

BUILDING A STONE WALL

Dry-stacked (that is, mortarless) stone walls are an old New England tradition that's now popular everywhere. Building one yourself is a cost-cutting way to add character and beauty to any landscape project, and in a waterside setting, the stones also provide a foothold for growing moss.

FOR THIS PROJECT YOU'LL NEED:

- Wooden stakes
- A small wooden mallet (for hammering stakes)
- String line
- Shovels
- Fine sand, called "rock screenings"
  (for walls over 3 feet high)
- Stone for walls
- Topsoil

WHEN SELECTING THE STONE:

There are four or five types of stone suitable for
making a dry-stacked wall and all are sold by
the pallet (one pallet will make a wall measuring
1 foot high by 30 feet long). Plain field
stone is the cheapest, but "Rustic Mountain"
and "Quarry Blue" are also options worth
considering. Prices vary from about $150 to $300
a pallet. For more detailed information, ask your
stone dealer.

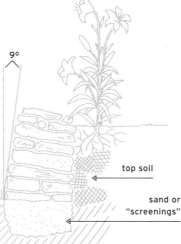

9°

top soil

sand or
"screenings"

STEP 1: Begin by selecting a site for the wall.
Keeping in mind that the finished wall should be about 18 inches
wide by whatever length you decide on, mark off these
dimensions with a series of stakes connected by string line.

STEP 2: Use a shovel to remove any grass and a few inches of
topsoil from the area lying within the marked-off stake lines.
Reserve topsoil for Step 5.

STEP 3: If the wall is going to be low (1 or 2 feet high) you can
go on to the next step. However, if it's to be higher (3 feet or
more) it's recommended that you remove an additional 6 inches
of topsoil, then replace that amount with sand (or rock
screenings) to make a foundation for the wall.

STEP 4: Starting at one end of the staked area, begin stacking
stones, being sure to keep the flat edges of the stone facing
front, and filling the gaps with smaller stone scraps as you go.
Note: As you build up the wall, it's very important that the
wall leans away from you at about an 8- or 9-degree angle (see
sketched illustration).

STEP 5: As the wall gets higher, fill it in from behind with
topsoil. Remember, perfection isn't a must—the look is supposed
to be rugged.

WATERSIDE ELEMENTS

When water and sky are the focal points, you don't want to hide them. What you do want are sturdy, mostly see-through pieces, including a provision for shade, some furnishings for entertaining, and maybe a water-themed *objet d'art* or two for bringing it all together, as we did here.

Nautically styled metal candle lanterns with glass walls to protect the flame from sea breezes are perfect for evening parties by the sea. Set them out on the table in pairs or hook up the handy ring for hanging.

Water-themed pieces are always good choices for ornamenting a seaside garden. Here, a sphere-shaped planter of terra-cotta is molded with a swirling pattern of seashells.

A welded-steel chair with a grid-patterned oval backrest and curlycued armrests looks like a Matisse sculpture. The bonus: its openwork construction allows you to see your waterside view.

A closeup of the cheerful fish-design tiles topping the dining table shown at left. Aside from adding an element of color, the tiles also have the practical advantage of being weatherproof.

The set piece includes a pergola we made by capping four welded-steel columns with vine-laced snow fencing. Beneath it are a welded-steel ladderback chair, a steel-legged table set with a cast-iron armillary, and two flanking papier-mâché flamingos.

Choose planters that are heavy enough to withstand maritime winds. That's no problem for this cement pot planted with its own steel topiary and set between two cement garden balls.

the urban garden

IF YOU LIVE in an urban environment (as our family does for a good part of the year), you probably agree with urban planner Lewis Mumford's claim that the city is "man's greatest work of art." At least, most of the time you do. Because, let's face it, even on the best of days, city life can be as exhausting as it is exhilarating, which explains why the urban garden has always been such a highly valued commodity.

The gardens in this chapter were photographed in Manhattan, but whatever city it grows in, an urban garden is the oasis we gravitate toward as a welcome respite from the city's concrete and cacophony. It's the quiet place we seek out for the simple, revitalizing pleasure of contemplating the cityscape or watching how falling snow contours a piece of statuary. In short, an urban garden is what softens the hard edges of urban living.

Yet like cities themselves, urban gardens are so tremendously varied that there's no set list of characteristics to describe them. As you'll see on the following pages, they offer a very personal statement, a reaction, I suspect, to the cookie-cutter anonymity that permeates much of city life. Under such conditions, the urban garden becomes a place where we can assert our individuality and

carve out a little private green world for ourselves.

Another explanation for the great variety in urban gardens has to do with their location and size. An urban retreat might be a penthouse rooftop, an apartment terrace, or the postage-stamp-sized backyard of a town house. In cities such as Miami, where urban sprawl is measured on the horizontal as well as the vertical, an urban garden might even be a comparatively large plot of land behind a detached house. Regardless of the variants, there is always a sense of boundaries to these gardens, which will inevitably determine their design.

Urns and other planters are a good case in point. If your urban (or suburban) plot is fairly large and has enough ground to accommodate plant materials, planters serve merely as additional decorative elements. But in every other type of urban garden, they provide the only soil for growing plants. In effect, they *are* your land and therefore essential.

The same goes for fencing. If your little bit of Eden happens to be high up on a penthouse rooftop where privacy isn't an issue, fencing is optional. In most other locations, fencing isn't just decorative; it's a necessity. An additional consideration when choosing fencing is air circulation. In the backyard gardens of brownstones and town houses, which are often bounded by the towering walls of adjacent buildings as well as by one or more adjoining yards, it's important to select fencing that does not inhibit the flow of air.

In most urban garden sites, lawns are nonexistent, so paving is another important consideration. If the garden is at ground level, your best bet is to choose a paving material—brick, cobblestone, tile, and so on—that complements the style of your house. If the garden is on a terrace or a roof, your choices may be limited by municipal building codes. In New York City, for example, an ordinance was recently passed that deals specifically with roof-garden paving. The reason: it was discovered that several buildings had suffered structural damage from rain and plant watering as a result of unsuitable garden paving that didn't allow for proper moisture absorption and drainage.

Seating—another consideration—depends on the location and the size of your space. Usually it's a matter of making sure that chairs and benches are properly scaled to the space and match your decorative theme. If your urban garden is very small but you like to entertain there, the question of seating is crucial. One good solution is banquette seating that hugs the enclosure walls of your garden, leaving the central space open. The banquette we built for our brownstone garden provides storage beneath the seats, creating an ideal cache for garden tools, portable lanterns, seat cushions, and whatever else I don't want to lug indoors or have no room for anywhere else.

When space is limited in your urban garden, you don't want to clutter it up, so opt for as few pieces as you need to make your garden functional. Keep plant materials simple and monochromatic, and use the same thematic style for all furniture, planters, and so on.

Because urban gardens are such inviting places to entertain guests, don't forget lighting. This might be no more than a simple string of clear Christmas tree lights or something more dramatic to spotlight, say, one striking piece of sculpture.

This brings up a final consideration, which is the need to establish a focal point in your garden. If you overlook the city, that spectacular panorama is your focal point; if not, you can easily create one by adding a wonderful splashing fountain to feast your eyes upon and help soothe your urban-weary senses.

urban romance

P am Scurry's terrace garden is all about romance in the sky. Because she loves to entertain, the garden also serves the functional purpose of providing her guests with plenty of seating and dining space, not to mention the added entertainment offered by the bird's-eye view of Manhattan's Central Park. As you look around, you find yourself surrounded by an Edwardian fantasy of lacy white wrought-iron furniture, urns, statuary, a fountain, and other delightful treasures peeking out of the greenery. In one particularly inviting corner of the garden, there's even a live crab-apple tree to provide the visitor with sun-dappled shade.

OPPOSITE **First-time visitors to the garden never fail to appreciate the delightful incongruity of Edwardian elegance and lacy wrought iron residing on a penthouse terrace in present-day New York.** BELOW **A bas relief cupid festoons a wall-mounted fountain that not only pleases the eye, but also helps filter out city noise.**

a penthouse
view

One of the best things about a penthouse garden is that the surrounding cityscape makes the garden feel as if it goes on forever, even when it isn't very big at all. Such is the case with this delightful New York City retreat overlooking an impressive expanse of the East River.

The design is restrained and spare, and the placement of ornaments is satisfyingly symmetrical. Serving as a kind of three-dimensional frontispiece for the spectacular view is an equally spectacular statue of two children riding a giant fish. The owner found the antique piece in Paris and had it regilded. We were so taken with the effect—and with the owner's custom of embellishing her planters to suit the season—that we photographed the garden in autumn and again in December when it was all decked out for Christmas.

BELOW Chrysanthemums and wheat declare the season on a sunny autumn day. RIGHT In December, spotlights made the gilded statue gleam amid a bountiful yuletide feast of fir boughs and pine cones.

urban with
attitude

Fashion designer Betsey Johnson's urban garden on lower Fifth Avenue is as recognizably "Betsey" as her clothes—which is to say it is bursting with vibrant color and pattern.

For years her collection of flea market finds has been the inspiration for many of her clothing designs; here, those same pieces—a mixture of country and kitsch, rustic and retro—are set up in casual still lifes throughout her garden, so that it looks like a glorious penthouse yard sale.

In this urban garden, statues of maidens form a straggly chorus line alongside statues of mermaids. Bistro chairs share space with a wind-peeled Adirondack chair and an old wheeled chaise draped, perhaps, with a vintage quilt or coverlet as insurance against the odd chilly summer night. In one corner sits a typical Betsey touch: cut flowers in an assortment of vases arranged on a weathered baker's rack. The effect of all this quirky chic invites a put-your-feet-up casualness that's the very essence of relaxation.

In the background, you can see the scaled-down skyline that typifies lower Manhattan. Up front is a job lot of furniture and objects comfortably scattered around several birch trees and a garden of annuals that come to life in April and May.

OPPOSITE A placid-looking cow's head sculpture looms over an "altar" vignette, with deity, candles, et al. Not your average garden decoration, but their delightful unexpectedness (and their effectiveness as a statement of the owner's unique style), exemplify what an urban garden can be about. ABOVE Statues of a man and maid gaze at one another in a flea-market Eden furnished with chaise longues and lavished with bright lilac paint. LEFT For Betsey Johnson, fabric isn't just a tool of her trade, it's a passion! So it's not unusual to find pieces of furniture casually draped with swaths of cloth for the sole purpose of adding pattern and color. BELOW, LEFT An arrangement of fresh flowers in assorted vases turns a trellis-walled corner into a dazzling flower-shop display. BELOW, RIGHT More collected items: a bevy of lovely little mermaids lounging on a garden shelf.

On the garden deck fronting Hayes's office is a feisty little potted plant that she moves from spot to spot in order to catch every precious ray of sunlight.

garden feats

Paula Hayes is an innovative artist whose medium happens to be urban gardens. In fact, if her landscape design business had a heraldic crest, the motto could be "against all odds," because she rises above any challenge to create thriving oases that are works of art.

One example of that ability is a serene little brownstone garden on the East Side of Manhattan. The ornamental paving, brick walls, and lovely wrought-iron entry gates (all legacies from the 1920s) echo similar enclosures found in New Orleans' French Quarter, a feature much appreciated by the present owners, who lived in that city before moving to New York. The only drawback: the site's limited supply of space and light. Hayes's solution was to install a chiaroscuro of shade-loving plants—including two climate-defying magnolias—that frames the garden and seems to double the size.

One of the best examples of Hayes's garden design ingenuity is the little deck space outside her office in lower TriBeCa. Surrounded by towering buildings, the garden site resembles the bottom of an air shaft: sunlight is available only briefly every day, and in colder months it barely shows up at all. Yet with the true grit of a New York gardener, she's managed to fashion a delightful green haven from such disparate elements as a collection of romantic topiaries, a rustic Adirondack chair, and a montage of outsized clay pots planted with a variety of greens that flourish in defiance of all reasonable expectations.

Not far from this West Side spot, there's a penthouse garden (complete with lap pool) whose focal point is a vintage brick wall capped by a slate pyramid roof. Hayes incorporated this wonderful element into the garden itself by covering the wall with trellises for wisteria that will bloom in profusion come spring.

The essential ornaments in this garden are the plants themselves, all hearty varieties that can stand up to the rooftop's high winds and strong sunlight. River birches are housed in boxes, and silver lace vines grow on a trellis that forms a see-through wall at one end of the garden. Most impressive is the sight of perennials sprouting from beds that were cleverly sunk beneath the penthouse garden's deck.

The deck itself is another testimonial to Hayes's talent for meeting a challenge. When faced with a city fire ordinance that restricts the use of wood decking to 25 percent of the floor space, she covered the rest with a patchwork of blue tiles by local artisan Dan Peterman, who made them from recycled, fire-retardant plastic. It was a case of invention answering necessity—resulting in the spectacular!

LEFT The establishing elements of this little brownstone garden, including gates, walls, and paving, are all legacies from the 1920s. But the space-opening plantings around its perimeter were the exclusive work of its designer, Paula Hayes. BELOW A stone finial adorns a corner of the garden's brick wall. BOTTOM One wonderful feature of the garden's mellowed brick wall is the circular cutout that opens the way for air and light while it frames the view of a lovely cast-iron bench in a neighboring yard.

OPPOSITE A penthouse terrace on Manhattan's West Side features the World Trade Center as background. The soil source for a mini-garden of plants is a large terra-cotta pot. RIGHT An interesting brick wall fills the roles of garden boundary and anchor for trellises that will bloom with wisteria vines in spring. BELOW, LEFT A sunflower shaped shower head is used for rinsing off the chlorine after a workout in the lap pool. BELOW, RIGHT Flowers erupt from Hayes's cleverly contrived sunken garden bed surrounded by a patchwork of floor-covering tiles.

countrified
urban

When the owner, a museum director in the central United States, accepted a new directorship in New York, he and his wife began an exhaustive search for a Manhattan apartment they could happily call home. After viewing seventy-two offerings, they finally found it: an upper Park Avenue penthouse with a beautiful wraparound terrace garden.

Penthouse it may be, but the character—both inside and out—says "country cottage," from the lavish use of white trellises on the garden walls to the lineup of boxy wooden planters with matching storage chest/garden seats and the addition of striped grocer's awnings over the windows.

The plant materials are as varied and plentiful as any in a country garden and feature a number of small trees, including two Japanese maples whose feathery red leaves fan out over a narrow walkway. There are the amenities of a cottage garden as well: just outside the glass-walled kitchen an herb garden grows in a collection of little pots on a corner-hugging baker's stand, all ready for the picking when needed.

One side of the penthouse apartment's wraparound terrace overlooks the fog-softened view of the Central Park reservoir. And for enjoying that privileged view in complete comfort, a stripe-padded Brown Jordan chaise.

OPPOSITE The apartment's dining area lives in a little glass house that's an extension of the kitchen. And, like all the best country kitchens, this one boasts an herb garden just outside the door. Here, the herbs grow in separate pots on the shelves of an iron baker's rack. RIGHT Fire escapes are an urban necessity, but the owners have added the country charm of geraniums growing in twin urns to embellish the entry space opening to it. BELOW, LEFT A cast-iron ram's head urn from China is the centerpiece for a dining table and chairs. BELOW, RIGHT A trellised wall (the kind so familiar to traditional country gardens) is fronted by a series of tulip fixtures that are turned on at night to illuminate a border of strawberry plants.

east river eden

For Cathryn Collins and Gerald Imber, M.D., Eden is a shady garden overlooking the East River just north of the United Nations building. In the near distance, lacy tree branches swoon lazily against the sky and tugboats can be heard calling to one another on a misty night. Adding to this tranquillity is the uncluttered simplicity of the garden itself. Its "bones" are the brick-paved spaces that curve around low-walled plant beds. Beyond that, ornamentation is minimal; just a few beautifully fashioned metal chairs, a sculpture or two, and, acting as focal points (the contributions of landscape architect Michael Trapp) are a ruined column and moss-covered rocks arranged in a cast-iron urn.

Such oases of peace and natural beauty, so rarely found within city confines, need little in the way of adornment. Here, all the elements, including a sleek-lined metal chaise, a ruined pillar, and a tree-hung lantern, reflect the simple serenity of the garden site itself.

ABOVE After years of friendly persuasion, the owners finally induced their garden designer to part with the striking ruined column that's now one of the site's primary focal points. ABOVE, RIGHT Michael Trapp's version of a rockery is a collection of moss-covered rocks piled into a graceful cast-iron urn. RIGHT The metal grid design of the furniture suggests a sophisticated take on trellising that's a subtle form of ornamentation in itself. OPPOSITE A carved stone Oriental head immersed in a lush bed of ivy.

CREATING A GARDEN BANQUETTE

When seating space is minimal, as it often is in an urban garden, you can
make the most of every square inch with a custom-built banquette. Ours
has a removable seat for storage and a backrest for comfort. Add cushions, push a table in front of it, and it's also a space-saving dining bench.

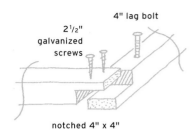

4" lag bolt

2½" galvanized screws

notched 4" x 4"

A WORD OF ADVICE: This isn't a project for beginners. But if need be, get someone to build it for you by following these instructions. Before your start, read through all the directions carefully. Also see page 200 for general wood-project guidelines.

FOR THIS PROJECT YOU'LL NEED:

- Pressure-treated wood (CCA), including four-by-fours for the basic framework, one-by-sixes for the vertical supports and slats, and one-by-ones to support the removable seat top (amounts will depend on the banquette length required)
- A power saw
- An electric screw gun
- Lag bolts (for attaching bench to brick or concrete paving and supporting walls)
- 2½-inch galvanized flat-head sheetrock screws (for attaching slats to frame)
- 3-inch-wide wood trim to cap top of backrest

STEP 1: Cut and notch four-by-fours as shown and secure with screws to make the frame for the base.

STEP 2: Attach base frame to pavement with lag bolts.

STEP 3: Cut wood slats from one-by-sixes and screw them side by side into the base frame from behind using 2½-inch screws.

STEP 4: Cut and notch four-by-fours as shown and secure with screws to make the frame (including vertical side supports) for the backrest and seat.

STEP 5: Positioning yourself between the vertical slats and the wall, screw vertical slats to backrest/seat frame.

STEP 6: Cut more vertical slats from one-by-sixes for backrest. From front, screw slats to backrest frame rail and to seat frame rail as shown. Screws at top and bottom of slats will be hidden by trim cap and removable seat respectively.

STEP 7: Construct removable seat covers from one-by-sixes as shown.

STEP 8: Screw lengths of one-by-ones one inch below top edge of the backrest/seat frame's seat rail as shown, and drop seat covers into place.

STEP 9: Cover top of backrest with wood trim and attach with screws.

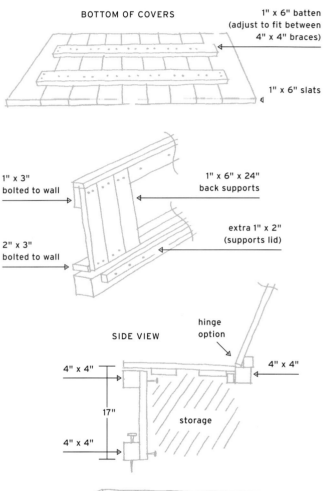

BOTTOM OF COVERS

1" x 6" batten (adjust to fit between 4" x 4" braces)

1" x 6" slats

1" x 3" bolted to wall

1" x 6" x 24" back supports

2" x 3" bolted to wall

extra 1" x 2" (supports lid)

SIDE VIEW

hinge option

4" x 4"

4" x 4"

17"

storage

4" x 4"

41"

17"

24"

Nowadays, wonderful fiberglass look-alikes of antique garden pieces are finding a ready market. One popular example is a two-tiered pedestal stone-look fountain topped with two cavorting cherubs.

Sleek lines and soft contours distinguish a pair of aluminum chairs and a tub, just what an urban garden needs for toning down the hard edges of building walls, paving, and boundary fences.

Because city gardens and summer parties go hand in hand, the folding bistro chair is an urban necessity for extra seating. These feature wood slats and aluminum frames.

This sleek metal armchair is a marriage between urban high-tech and traditional Windsor. The advantage of this union is that it combines comfort with all-weather practicality.

A great find for a sun-drenched penthouse or terrace garden is a cast-iron umbrella-frame topiary. You provide the growing vines, and it supplies some welcome shade wherever you happen to need it.

The background interest is Manhattan's Fifty-Ninth Street Bridge and a sphere-topped tower sculpture by Dagney Duvall. To the fore, an exotic statue dangles its feet in a circular fountain. And in between are a settee and two chairs of weather-safe mahogany, and two large, stone-look square planters.

URBAN ELEMENTS

City gardens are as individual as their owners, so with that variety in mind, we've assembled a few essentials that could be considered your basic urban starter kit: that is, furnishings with a clean-lined sophistication that would fit into most urban garden spaces, and complement just about any style you fancy.

the romantic garden

IN THE LATE EIGHTEENTH CENTURY, Jean-Jacques Rousseau said, "I felt before I thought," and in those five words summed up the spirit of a cultural concept that would knock the classical ideal right off its Doric pedestal. In the arts, the revolution called "romanticism" was characterized chiefly by a highly subjective and emotional view of nature and by a nostalgia for the past, or what the German writer E.T.A. Hoffmann described as "an infinite longing."

Translated into the language of garden design, romanticism often meant lush hangings of seemingly untamed greenery punctuated by the requisite piece of damaged statuary, maybe a moss-covered column or two, and—because the past so nostalgically longed for was usually medieval—an artistically ruined Gothic arch. The effect was deliciously melancholic. It was mystical. Sometimes, it was even exotic (Oriental structures, such as pagodas, were greatly admired). All of it was as different from cerebral classicism as it was possible to be.

Today we're seeing a kind of romantic revival that embraces many of the original elements but with one significant difference: Our nostalgia isn't for the distant past but for a far more recent one —our own. As a consequence of that single shift

in perspective, the inspirational sources for romantic garden design—and for the use of garden ornaments—are practically limitless.

With this new way of thinking, such a garden might be based on, say, a pastoral drawing first encountered in a treasured book from childhood. It might be inspired by a stage set remembered from a favorite vintage movie, or by a distinctive structural style once seen while in a foreign country and never forgotten. The new romanticism is a uniquely personal vision that emerges from something embedded deeply within us, and in that regard it captures the original spirit of the old.

One obvious advantage of this particular approach is that there are no steadfast rules to stifle your innate creativity. The romantic garden is pretty much whatever you want to make it. Another plus is that it doesn't tie you down to one specific style. If, like many of us, your taste happens to be eclectic—say, you love the French countryside and Japanese teahouses and have a special affinity for the pioneer rusticism of the Old West—you can create little vignettes based on as many themes as your space will allow.

Having established the answer to "What is a romantic garden?" the next question is "How can I create one?" Given freedom of choice, How do we go about creating a garden that's uniquely personal and still recognizably romantic? This is important because in spite of the variety of romantic gardens, there are common elements that distinguish all of them.

For one thing, there's a softness to the romantic look; there's nothing high-tech or hard-edged about it. But because a good deal of its impact comes from intrinsically solid ornaments—benches, statues, fences, urns, quaint little garden houses—you have to reconcile the softness and the solidity. The best way to do that is with the careful selection and placement of plant materials.

When you put a plant in a pot, or set a potted plant on the seat of a chair or a bench, you immediately soften the contours of all the ornaments placed in that particular area. Another trick is to include flowers and plants that are characteristically feathery, rounded, and languid. These could be mounds of hydrangea spilling over a picket fence, or masses of delicate New Dawn roses blanketing a low porch roof. If you happen to live in a warm-weather region such as Miami, where several of our romantic gardens are located, you can plant miniature ficus or some other fast-growing vine that will cover a wire fence or a stone

column to mellow the severity of these surfaces.

The inclusion of water is another surefire way to romanticize your garden. Be it a pool, a fountain, a chuckling stream, or a man-made pond, there's something about the presence of water in an outdoor setting that evokes an almost reflexive emotional response in us. Perhaps it's the yielding coolness of water when we trail our fingers in it, or the calming sound of it in motion, or the way it reflects the changing light. Whatever the reason, there's no doubting its power to charm us.

Finally, we can ask: "Who is the romantic gardener?" A true romantic gardener probably has an innate affection for earlier times and other places. The person might be an enthusiastic collector of scrapbooks, postcards, and old photographs, or someone who keeps a well-thumbed list of all the best flea markets and whose minivan automatically brakes at yard sales. Or the person might be a world traveler whose favorite vacation pastime includes searching out new garden ideas and ornaments—or even the weekend artisan who likes to turn scrapyard finds into unique pieces of garden art.

Recognize yourself in any of this? If so, chances are you're a romantic gardener at heart.

scenic
fantasies

Landscape artist Lisa Stamm and her architect husband, Dale Booher, run a thriving landscape design business. Prospective clients who ask to see examples of their work are given a guided tour of the couple's own spectacular nine-acre property on Shelter Island, New York. As a showcase for the range of their design styles, it can't be topped. Yet the thematic vignettes they've created add up to a very personal space with "romantic" written all over it.

Because Stamm and Booher are zealous travelers, their garden themes include re-creations of favorite spots they've seen, as well as places only imagined, so that visitors have the dreamlike impression of moving through a series of stage sets. There's an exotically roofed lean-to (a tribute to similar structures encountered in Thailand) where guests can relax with drinks before a cozy autumnal campfire. In another spot is a pergola-shaded composition of two wire café chairs and a table that instantly conjures up an image of southern France. In still another, there's a delightfully rural man-made pond with marsh plants, a dock, and an old rowboat: Opie's Mayberry comes to life.

It's a showcase, yes, but also a joint labor of love to which both partners contributed their own expertise—which makes it romantic in both senses of the word!

Suggestions of antiquity—a ruined column in a circle of flowers, the apparition of a temple on a distant hill—set the mind on a dreamy journey back to ancient Greece.

LEFT A venerable tree circumscribed by an old wooden seat where pub patrons might sit to enjoy a pint or two is a traditional sight in English villages. Here, reinforced with the addition of two Adirondack chairs, it's just as inviting of rest and conversation as the originals on which it's based. BELOW, LEFT Take two classic wire chairs and a bistro table, set them up beneath a shady pergola, and suddenly you're in a small café somewhere in rural France. BELOW A little antique table with three topiary plants in terra-cotta pots makes an attractive vignette on the walkway beneath the veranda roof. OPPOSITE The ruined temple (also glimpsed on the previous page) is a good lesson in fantasy spinning made easy. Achieved by the simple expedient of connecting two old vine-spiraled columns with a horizontal pediment, it's a magic trick that produces a vanished dream of classical Greece.

ABOVE A primitive garden bench
constructed from stone slabs rests
between two shade-giving trees.
ABOVE, RIGHT A fantastical lean-to,
which the owners copied from similar
structures they saw in Thailand, is an
ideal spot for relaxing or entertaining.
RIGHT The vine-arched gate with
its faux balustrade of shaped flat-wood
slats is another charming example of
Booher's handiwork. OPPOSITE Setting
a stone obelisk in the middle of
a field path is not just an interesting
visual comment, it's also an obstacle
deliberately placed in the walker's
path so that he or she is forced to stop,
look, and appreciate its simple lines
and weathered surfaces.

garden
memorabilia

Antiques dealer Suzanne Lipschitz wasn't always a gardener, but when confronted with the barren lawns at the front and back of her newly purchased Miami house, she immediately launched a green-up campaign. Now, eight years later, the house is all but hidden by the miniature tropical forest she planted, nurtured, and, in the process, became quite knowledgeable about.

Drawing on the same creative talent that infuses her shop, the well-known Second Hand Rose in Manhattan, she carved out a series of romantic spaces in her garden and filled them with her favorite things. These range from a collection of religious statues to a colorfully painted fountain to boxed bromeliads that sit upon sweet little tree-trunk chairs. These pieces were not necessarily expensive—many were flea-market finds—but seeing them tucked in their tropical setting elicits the same kind of innocent pleasure that a child would feel on discovering hidden treasure.

OPPOSITE A female nude watches over a cement garden path scored to resemble a crazy quilt. On either side of it, a mini-rain forest of tropical plants thrives on what was once barren lawn. ABOVE, RIGHT Bromeliads in a slatted box sit in the lap of a rustic chair. RIGHT Rescued from an old movie house, an elaborately painted fountain now serves as a stage prop for the owner's collection of religious statues.

ornamented rooms

Folly is an English architectural term for a personally interpreted garden structure. On this Bedford, New York, property, the folly—an utterly delightful cross between a pagoda and a country train station—serves as an impressive viewing stand overlooking the tennis court.

Aside from that utilitarian function, however, owner Victoria Michealis has also made it the anchor for a series of trellis-walled garden rooms. Within every enclosure, and scattered throughout the property, are single, isolated ornaments—a stone birdbath, a ruined column, a gracefully carved urn—that serve as kinds of suzerains ruling their own separate spaces in majestic solitude. The resulting effect is serene, uncluttered, and—in melancholy autumn especially—the very definition of romantic.

With its lush vines and surrounding woodland, the garden's romantic aura is chiefly established by the setting itself. But when seen against the subtle glories of autumn, architectural nuances emerge, drawing the eye to ornamental details such as the pagoda curve of a roof, the handsome gridwork of a fence, and the ball finials marking the place of the tennis court's little swing gate.

ABOVE An antique stone baptismal font enjoys stately solitude in a woodsy clearing. ABOVE, RIGHT The folly in situ. With its compelling roof, supporting pillars, and open-wall construction, this key garden structure is a natural gathering spot for warm-weather entertainments, for watching tennis, or for just enjoying the view. RIGHT An old column is framed by the viney arch in a trellis wall. OPPOSITE When a single ornament, like this antique cast-iron birdbath, is centrally placed within an enclosed space, it not only gains importance but also allows the viewer to savor the details without distraction.

rural romanticism

There's a garden in Bridgehampton, Long Island, where visitors experience the pleasantly disorienting sensation of having somehow wandered into rural Kansas. The owners of this romantic fantasy are Peri Wolfman and her husband, Charlie Gold, the names behind Wolfman-Gold, a popular decorative home furnishings store in Manhattan's SoHo district.

When these New Yorkers wanted to re-create a piece of the unspoiled Midwest on the grounds of their weekend retreat, they called in landscape designers Lisa Stamm and Dale Booher, whose own romantic garden was featured earlier in this chapter. Wolfman and Gold's choice of theme wasn't a random one. As it happened, there was already an old barn on the property, standing empty and in need of repair. Reinvigorated, it's now a studio-cum-pool house that anchors the garden's farm-country theme.

Another lucky circumstance was that the owners' property line ran smack up against a neighboring farmer's cornfield. Realizing the potential of this arrangement, Booher came up with the idea of installing a big weathered farm gate as an "entryway" to the field. Suddenly, those vast acres of corn became a visual extension of the couple's more limited space, and looked for all the world as if they belonged to it.

LEFT **A rusticated stick tower upholds a birdhouse while providing a topiary frame for plants growing at the tower's base.** OPPOSITE **The addition of an old farm gate visually appropriates the expanse of a neighboring cornfield.**

OPPOSITE Filled with water, these galvanized washtubs are handy for washing soil from fresh-picked veggies. NEAR RIGHT Flowers bloom in a medium of sphagnum moss. FAR RIGHT A wire trash bin turned storage container for terra-cotta pots. BELOW, LEFT A topiary sprouts in front of a rural fence. BELOW, RIGHT A wheeled tub for a multitude of garden jobs.

fairy-tale romance

There's rustic rustic, and there's romantic rustic. This Sagaponack, Long Island, garden definitely falls into the latter category. Its success as a storybook fantasy is due entirely to the expertise of its owners, David Seefer and Njaere McCrea Zohn, who are also husband-and-wife proprietors of the Bayberry Nursery in nearby Amagansett.

Whereas the ornamental materials themselves—mostly rough-hewn stone and unpainted wood—contribute a rural simplicity to the overall look, the plant materials serve to soften and romanticize it. For example, a spare-lined picket fence enclosing a garden space is contoured by pillowy masses of hydrangea growing through it or drifting over it. A geometrically sculptured wooden bench that occupies a corner is surrounded by an arc of feathery flowers and vines. And where stones wall in a border plot, they barely contain the burgeoning mounds of flowers and plants spilling out from behind them.

This clever contrasting of forms and textures can be seen all over the property, but only by visitors who make themselves conscious of it. Most are content to ignore the stratagem, and simply enjoy the illusion.

While the wide entry gate is basically rustic, its individual poles are graduated to arc gently upwards at the sides. Result: the effect is less rigid and made softer still by the pillowy clusters of hydrangea hanging over it.

ABOVE Here the dipping arc of a pine
gate relieves the solidity of the
gate itself and makes a nice contrast
against the precise horizontals
of the tall hedges surrounding it.
RIGHT The cross pieces of a
rugged pergola are anchor for (and
mellowed by) the vine stems
twining gracefully around them.

ABOVE Another example of the arc triumphant. Here, a series of them helps to relax the perpendicular lines of a corner garden bench.
BELOW Not the wolves of fairy tale, but a trio of sculptured coyote pups placed on the verge of a field.

AGING A STONE PLANTER

For many gardeners, mold and age spots are to stone ornaments what patina is to antique furniture—a sign of both age and character. If you're one who's always been partial to that very desirable effect, you can age a stone planter or terra-cotta pot in no time by using one of the following methods.

TO GROW MOLD ON A PLANTER: All you need to do is smear it with (or soak it in) a spore-growing medium such as yogurt, beer, old fish-tank water, manure, or Miracle-Gro solution. Rub the medium-treated planter with a chunk of live moss; then set the pot in a cool, damp, shady place. In a few weeks the piece will be moldy.

TO ARTIFICIALLY AGE A POT: You can use a wash made from two parts latex exterior paint (or latex stucco paint) to one part water. The paint color you choose will depend on the effect you're trying to achieve. White will add a powdery finish to terra-cotta; moss green on cement will make it look moldy; and blue-green will add an oxidized copper patina to terra-cotta or cement. Just brush the paint mixture onto the pot, then rub it off with a damp sponge so that residue is left in the cracks and depressions. You can also try using more than one color. For example, apply white, then moss green, then black, rubbing off between coats as just described.

TO AGE POTS MADE OF FIBERGLASS OR PLASTIC: Substitute oil-based paint for water-based, and dilute with turpentine or paint thinner. Do wear rubber gloves for this, because working with oil-based paint can get messy.

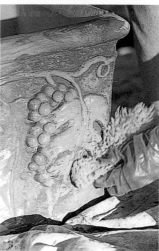

You need a dining set anyway; why not make it a great one? In that category: a round, sunburst-design table made of teak wood and painted steel, with matching folding chairs.

A striking Victorian wrought-iron chandelier hangs from our pavilion roof. The twelve Pyrex-glass vases use wicks and candle oil to cast a soft glow on romantic dinners for two.

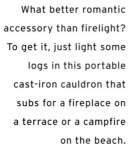

What better romantic accessory than firelight? To get it, just light some logs in this portable cast-iron cauldron that subs for a fireplace on a terrace or a campfire on the beach.

Every garden patio should have a versatile wrought-iron party tub that's a potential fire pit/planter/drinks icer/fountain, or just about anything else you can think to make of it.

It's the same pergola now sitting on the dock of the bay. We moved it to show its surprising portability. In as little as 20 minutes, it can be set up or taken apart for easy storage.

The courtyard of our weekend house features a structural pavilion that we adorned with lights and set up to establish the sense of an outdoor room for romantic garden dining.

ROMANTIC ELEMENTS

When mapping out your romantic garden, the operative word should be "soft": soft lighting for evening entertaining, ornaments with soft-lined detailing, furniture with lots of gentle contours and curves in its design.

the rustic garden

IT'S EASY TO IMAGINE that Daniel Boone could have created this kind of garden for himself if only he'd managed to find the time. The rustic garden encompasses a secluded woodland setting with tangles of wildflowers and vines and primitive, rough-hewn structures and furnishings with everything about it looking as unpretentious and honest as the day is long.

Rustic design was far more widely spread and goes a lot farther back than the early American frontier. We know, for example, that gardens in fourteenth-century China featured architectural elements made from roots, and in the 1700s equally rustic garden structures existed in England, France, and Italy, as they did in just about every other country in the world.

What this suggests is that even as "sophisticated" garden style emerged and developed, as it did from about 2500 B.C. onward, rustic was always right there. It was not always acknowledged as a valid garden style, perhaps, but it was undeniably present.

The reason for rustic design's status as a kind of stylistic stepchild becomes evident when you remember that "style" has traditionally originated in the upper classes before gradually descending to the lower, as was the case with classical and

romantic garden styles. But rustic came from the common man, from farmers and laborers whose only design source was their own imagination. Unskilled in the cabinetmaker's art—and, in the more isolated areas, probably totally innocent of its very existence—they fashioned whatever they needed from the materials close at hand: tree trunks and branches, roots and vines, rocks and stones, even animal bones and antlers. These are the same materials that rustic garden furnishings are made from to this day.

Between the end of the American Civil War and the beginning of the Great Depression, the polarized coexistence of rustic and sophisticated gradually began to change. In that fascinating period of growth and prosperity, vast fortunes were being made by railroad barons, industrial magnates, and financiers whose power bases lay in New York and Boston. In summer, when these wealthy urbanites wanted to escape the punishing heat and social torpidity of the city, they and their entire families headed for the unspoiled mountain woodlands. The camplike enclaves and rustic gardens they built for themselves were mostly the products of untrained local labor who used time-honored traditional methods. More sophisticated craftsmen would later add their own refinements, giving rise to several different schools of rustic design. But by then, "roughing it" (albeit with servants in tow) had become the fashion, and rustic garden design was finally being recognized as a legitimate style of its own.

Today, extraordinary rustic garden structures can still be seen in areas such as the Adirondacks, where the look became so popular that "rustic style" is often referred to as "Adirondack style," and where the famous Adirondack chair was created. The Catskills were another popular site for these early recreation camps and for large resorts such as Mohonk Mountain House, where guests can still stroll through spacious grounds filled with wonderful examples of rustic garden style. One structure of particular note at Mohonk is a two-story summerhouse which was modeled on designs by Andrew Jackson Downing, the same nineteenth-century landscape architect responsible for the lovely rustic structures still to be seen in New York City's Central Park.

What I love most about rustic gardens is their look of having simply grown out of the woodsy surroundings—which, in a very real sense, they have. When you see a gazebo made from twigs and branches, you may at first mistake it for a tree. Or you suddenly discover that a fallen log is really a bench or a hollowed-out planter.

There's an earthy naturalness to the rustic garden that's practically the antithesis of the classical. Whereas the latter aims for a pristine ideal, rustic tends toward the asymmetrical, the imperfect, the irregular. Rustic furniture looks as if it was cobbled together by a family of woodland elves; even manufactured pieces have an unfinished, handmade quality. If a chair or a table is painted, the paint will usually be peeling to show earlier incarnations in the colored layers beneath. In this regard, rustic is much like American country.

Though plant materials aren't a major focus in the rustic garden, they are important to it. Your wisest choices are hardy wildflowers, vines, mosses, and wild grasses that can withstand the filtered sunlight and extremes of cold indigenous to the mountainous woodland settings where these gardens are commonly found.

Down-home touches are key. Instead of burnished vases and obelisks, you're more likely to see terra-cotta pots, rusted garden tools, dented watering cans, and vintage baskets—unpretentious pieces that call up images of a simpler existence in an earlier time.

adirondack retreat

In true Adirondack tradition, this impressive property unfolds over several hundred acres of woods and meadows interlaced with walking paths. Some of these paths follow the curve of the lake, which comes with its own tiny bridge-connected island. Other paths wind their way through a rustic garden of folk-art sculptures.

There's an unwritten imperative in rustic garden design that says: Wherever you need to improve on nature, do it naturally. Here, the owners have done exactly that. When they wanted to create a small plateau alongside a running stream, they faced it with a low wall of rocks. When they needed a stairway to connect the house area with the lake below it, they chiseled out a cascade of wide, shallow steps, then added untrimmed logs for risers and stacked flat stones to form the flanking walls. When they required a special planter to hold a miniature garden of ivy and impatiens, they chose the hollowed-out trunk of a dead tree. It now lies in a shady spot looking as earthy and uncontrived as nature itself.

OPPOSITE A mosaic arrangement of natural branches forms the backrest of a bench. ABOVE, RIGHT In rustic gardens, nature provides ornaments such as this hollow log used as a planter. RIGHT Matching the earthiness of its setting is a birdbath fashioned from a chiseled-out stone slab on a pedestal.

More rustic additions that mimic the natural landscape. OPPOSITE A stairway with log risers and unmortared stone walls that connects the house above with the lakefront below. For adornment, long wooden planters were set onto the "railings," then filled with assorted flora. ABOVE Arches and Xs pattern a log fence separating the lawn from a wildflower garden. It's just one of many imaginative fence designs found in the rustic style. RIGHT The little wood-slat bridge was erected to link the estate with a tiny island that the owners visit for family picnics. BELOW One section of the garden features a smooth lawn dappled with a wonderful collection of folk art sculptures depicting creatures of the wild—like this fanciful metal rendering of a giant spider.

rustic
interpretations

The gardens you see here are the creative work of landscape designer Craig Socia, whose East Hampton—based business serves clients throughout the surrounding area. One reason for the success of the business has to do with his special talent and love for constructing rough-hewn pergolas of logs, branches, and vines—one-of-a-kind structures found in many of the spaces he's designed.

But Socia has another talent as well, and that is his ability to use rustic style in subtle, almost impressionistic ways that hint at other traditional themes. For example, to landscape the area around a swimming pool, he erected a pergola with rough log columns softened by leafy vines. The roof is left open to the sky, so it suggests the classical look of a ruined temple. When designing the garden for a little Hansel and Gretel cottage, he included log fences and gates that are as romantic—and rustic—as the house.

Socia sometimes uses a pergola to unify a garden. One such instance was a rustic version of monastic-garden design (shown on the opening pages of this chapter) that divided the flower bed into four small plots separated by slate pathways. By itself the garden was pretty, but with the addition of a pergola, it became sun-dappled, cozy, and irresistibly inviting.

ABOVE, LEFT A woodsy armchair fashioned from branches and vines. LEFT An antique iron gate roughly tied to tree-stump posts. OPPOSITE A primitive gate Socia made to span a stone-paved path that ambles through the garden.

a garden
for all seasons

In Austerlitz, New York, there's a small garden high on a ridge overlooking a mountain valley. Though it looks like it's been there forever, the idea of it didn't occur to owner Elizabeth Diggs until her daughter's wedding was held on the site and she realized what an ideal spot it would be for a garden. Inspired by the twig gardens that famed horticulturist Marco Polo Stefano created at Wave Hill in the Bronx, she designed a rustic fenced-in space featuring a lovely arbor created by her co-owner, Emily McCully.

In summer, the garden is awash in antique roses, but even in snowy winter it's a beautiful spot for serene walks and for watching the spectacular sunsets that gild the surrounding mountains.

ABOVE, LEFT A rugged, vine-thatched arbor that co-owner McCully tacked onto a corner of the fence-enclosed garden. LEFT Ornaments made in true rustic style will always be unique. Example: this singular garden chair constructed from remnants of milled wood. OPPOSITE Curved vine branches span the fence of a paddock area between the house and the garden. FOLLOWING PAGES An overview of the rectangular ridge-top garden in its beautiful mountain-valley setting.

BUILDING A TRELLIS

For other garden styles, a trellis might be traditionally designed or an architectural flight of fancy. For rustic, however, you want to reduce the concept of "trellis" to its basics: a simple structure of wood slats screwed together in a grid, which exactly describes the how-to project shown here.

BEFORE YOU START, read through all the directions. Also see page 200 for general wood-project guidelines. The trellis shown is 8 feet high and 42 inches wide, although you can modify the directions to accommodate any size you need.

FOR THIS PROJECT YOU'LL NEED:

- One-by-two redwood, including:

    Three 8-foot lengths (for verticals)

    Six 42-inch lengths (for horizontals)

    Six 5-inch lengths (to support the trellis on the wall and create space for plant growth)

- About 3 dozen 1½-inch-long galvanized flat-head wood screws
- A tape measure and pencil
- A wood saw
- An electric drill
- A manual (or electric) screwdriver
- If your wall is brick or concrete, you'll also need a masonry drill and expansion plugs to attach brackets

STEP 1: Lay the three 8-foot lengths on the ground vertically (wide side facing up) so they're parallel and 8 inches apart.

STEP 2: Lay the six 42-inch pieces horizontally across the vertical strips to form a grid whose openings are exactly 8 inches square. The squares around the perimeter will be open. When the horizontals are all in position, pencil along the top and bottom edges of each to mark their placement on the verticals.

STEP 3: With all the strips in place, screw the horizontals to the verticals at the center of each contact point.

STEP 4: Stain the finished trellis as well as the six 5-inch supporting blocks and let dry.

STEP 5: Place the trellis against the wall as a guide, then mark the wall at the top and bottom of the trellis's three verticals. Position the supporting blocks vertically so that when the trellis is in place, the blocks will be all but invisible behind it.

STEP 6: Secure the blocks to the wall with screw or expansion plugs, then screw the trellis to the blocks.

RUSTIC ELEMENTS

The cardinal rule of rustic: Opt for ornaments made from natural materials (preferably as found in their original state) so that they mesh with the surrounding landscape. But even within those parameters, the look can run the range from heavily primal all the way to lightheartedly quirky.

A primal-looking pyramid stone planter was constructed like a rugged dry-stack stone wall. It's a piece that Socia bought for a song from an artisan he discovered in Michigan.

This unusual cement planter is studded with shells. Small oblong-shaped ornaments like this one are especially handy for decorating a long table or the top of a boundary wall.

The metal chair, a suitably rustic-looking antique, has a vertical-slat backrest and springy hoop armrests connected to the rail supports so that it moves like a rocker.

Here's a primitive version of a club chair made of twigs, branches, and vines. It's the quintessence of rustic design, which means it's rugged, witty, and utterly unique.

Rustic one-of-a-kind pieces sit under a pergola that Craig Socia created for a client in Georgica, New York.

Another example of rustic wit is this steep-gabled birdhouse wrapped with vines and perched atop a little three-legged plant stand that also doubles as a side table.

the gallery garden

DURING THE PLANNING STAGES of this book, we hadn't thought of including a chapter on gallery gardens. But by the time Chuck and I had begun our photographing, we realized that several of the gardens we were seeing contained unusual pieces of great value. These ranged from antique urns and statues to original sculptural art to rare garden structures and furniture of such fine distinction as to merit the label "museum quality."

Often, one or two examples of this caliber of ornament determined the style of the garden that housed them, and we show these gardens in various chapters throughout the book. But sometimes, we would come across entire collections of notable works, displayed in surroundings that seemed to have been expressly designed to showcase them.

It soon became obvious that most of these gallery gardens had a number of factors in common. First and foremost, their owners are passionate collectors of fine art. This is reflected in the quality of work that decorates their homes as well as their gardens. As a rule, these collectors bring an informed appreciation to the particular periods, styles, and design nuances of the objects they collect. They happily spend months, even years, tracking down finds. One example of this perseverance is a collection of Victorian French wire garden chairs shown later in this chapter. An impressive assemblage in itself, it becomes doubly so when we learn that the owner searched out and acquired all of these extraordinary pieces separately over a long period of time.

Other elements linking these gardens have to do with their acreage as well as their design. Almost invariably, the grounds are extensive. Lawns, hedges, and trees are beautifully manicured and exquisitely maintained. Because green is to a gallery garden what white is to a gallery wall —a neutral canvas for the display of art—plant materials are secondary in importance and, therefore, in most instances kept very simple and monochromatic. Masses of bright colors are rarely seen in this type of garden. Wherever flowering plants do appear, they're usually unobtrusive and noncompetitive. Clearly, in this type of garden, the starring roles belong to the ornaments themselves.

Although we describe these pieces as being museum quality, some weren't always regarded that way. This is especially true of the Victorian and later vintages of architectural ornament once found on city buildings and in streets and parks. Until the last few decades or so, Americans didn't place much value on their architectural heritage.

Before we came to appreciate our treasures, many fine examples were lost to the wrecker's ball or abandoned to the ravages of time and weather in vast municipal graveyards.

Photographs, paintings, and old drawings reveal how our cities looked fifty to a hundred years ago. Study them closely and you begin to see the decorative detail that gave such distinction to our urban architecture and furnishings. There were ornately designed arms and legs for park benches, vine-patterned cast-iron supports for lampposts, and strikingly lifelike renderings of figures, faces, animals, and plants to adorn entryways and facades of buildings.

Although the makers of architectural ornament remained anonymous, their works could be seen everywhere. Because the excellence that we so prize in these pieces today was then the accepted norm—and so, consequently, was taken for granted—their casual sacrifice in the name of progress became almost inevitable. Looking back from our own more enlightened age, it's easy to condemn the blind destruction of the past, but the problem lay in the sheer ubiquity of these artisanal designs. Only when such craftsmanship became rare did people begin to appreciate how wonderful it really was.

Of course, it is true that there were always a few visionary souls with the eye to see the beauty of these ornaments and the wit to preserve them. And so you can discover surviving examples of this outdoor art in unexpected places in many older towns and cities. You can also see them in garden museums and in art museums with annexes for displaying garden ornaments. It's reassuring to know that a great many of these and other valuable garden artifacts have also been gathered together and preserved in private collections, as demonstrated on the pages that follow.

Even if your property isn't estate-sized and your art budget isn't in the Fortune 500 class, you can create a small-scale gallery garden of your own. It's just a matter of keeping things simple, with a bit of lawn and a monochromatic selection of plants. As for ornaments, you can find all kinds of reasonably priced architectural remnants in salvage yards, antiques shops, and garden shops that specialize in such decorative bygones. You might even call your local parks commission to see if it has old iron fencing, benches, fountains, and the like left over from recent renovation projects. Wherever you find ornamental art, choose only pieces you will enjoy looking at for a long time to come.

designer's gallery

Visiting Bill Blass's spacious property in Washington, Connecticut is like walking into an English park with acres of meandering lawns, plants, and trees. Encountering one or another of the sculptures that ornament these grounds —an exquisitely carved stone chair nestled in the woods, a spiral-pedestaled sundial overlooking a grassy terrace—reveals their absolute rightness in being exactly where they are. More than having been carefully positioned in a particular spot, they seem to have grown out of it and existed there forever.

Not unexpectedly, all the pieces are utterly unique and interesting. Blass rescued the nineteenth-century figures of actors from London's old Haymarket Theatre when it was being demolished. The Greek chorus of stone philosophers' busts, which are lined up like noble sentries before a stand of pines, came from one of Main Line Philadelphia's famous gardens.

Among the antiquities are newcomers as well. A starkly modern bas-relief of a male torso, for example, dates to around 1960. Yet somehow this mixed company lives together in easy comfort, as quality pieces always do, whatever their age.

OPPOSITE Actors' figures from a 19th-century London theater, now "resting" on the Blass estate.
ABOVE, RIGHT An unusually carved antique stone chair in the woods.
RIGHT A gracefully curved antique stone park bench is perfectly placed for viewing the landscape.

OPPOSITE Discovered in a
Georgetown antiques shop, this
collection of upstanding (and
outstanding) philosophers' busts
originally graced a famous garden
in old Philadelphia. ABOVE An
octagonal antique urn positioned
on a squared stack of stones.
ABOVE, RIGHT The circular bas
relief of a male torso (a sculpture
from Yugoslavia) is one of the
few moderns in a collection
of antiquities. RIGHT Overlooking
a manicured terrace is a
beautifully simple antique sundial
on a pedestal of spiraled stone.

eclectic collections

Gil Shapiro is one of those foresighted people who help rescue architectural art from oblivion. As cofounder and co-owner of Urban Archaeology, a New York City paradise for collectors of such work, he gets first crack at some of its best examples, which along with other valuable acquisitions, now ornament his garden on Long Island.

As in many gallery gardens, his collection contains a mix of styles and periods culled from a number of sources. For example, a zinc female figure that came from one of the nineteenth-century New York cast-iron buildings for which Jordan Mott was famous shares garden room with a pair of carved marble dogs whose former home was an English castle.

Shapiro insists that the criterion for most of his choices is that they be functional as well as decorative. For example, a lacy cast-iron gazebo allows family members to sit and enjoy the view, and an unusual Victorian cast-iron twig fence acts as the enclosure to his pool. But, in fact, the entire collection serves to delight the eye and recall an ideal from the past. What could be more functional than that?

Artisan art includes a delicate-looking gazebo and a superb folk-art grapevine fence. Remarkably, both of these cast-iron pieces from 1870s America still retain their original paint. FOLLOWING PAGES, LEFT The carved marble dogs, signed and dated 1810, are from an English castle. RIGHT A Victorian zinc figure designed by Jordan Mott.

garden
artifacts

A folly, as any Anglophile will tell you, is an English term for a whimsical garden structure, but Manhattanites know it as the name of a marvelous shop where Susan Lyall and her business partner, David Easton, sell rare garden ornaments that she scours much of Europe to find.

Some of those finds are displayed in three of the locations where Lyall spends a good deal of her time when not on buying trips. One is the Folly showroom, a space roomy enough to house such wonderful rarities as a seventeenth-century English bell tower.

Another display site is Lyall's penthouse garden on New York City's Upper East Side. This cozy rooftop space is filled with hardy flowering plants that poke through hanging antique wire baskets and entwine the legs of Victorian benches and chairs.

Finally, there's the gallery garden itself, a parklike estate of grassy rolling hills in Philadelphia where we took a few liberties in mixing some of the garden artifacts from Folly with antiques that Lyall already has in her garden. Among the former: the set of outsized cast-iron obelisks seen on page 147. Among the latter: a pair of exquisite shallow urns, a rare curved iron bench, and—appropriately enough—a *folly,* sitting majestically on a low plant-scaped mound.

Like all gallery gardens, this one
spotlights the ornaments themselves.
Here, the starring role belongs
to a rare 19th-century iron bench
whose curved back perfectly
fits the contours of an ancient tree.

ABOVE Lyall's New York penthouse garden is another delightful repository for her European finds. Among them: a sweet little Victorian settee and a huge, flower-filled basket vase. LEFT On the Philadelphia estate, a splendid pair of shallow cast-iron urns decorates the enclosure walls of a stairway. BELOW, LEFT The Folly owner's folly, with its Shanghai-hat roof and multipaned octagonal walls, rules on its own little landscaped mound. BELOW Beauty and the beasts. The cows may be oblivious to the lady's charms, but we weren't, which is why we photographed them behind this antique stone figure to demonstrate the contrast between brute nature and the finely-carved statue that's nothing less than art. OPPOSITE Another of Lyall's noteworthy rarities is this antique metal bench with its own built-on footrest.

a reposeful gallery

This serene garden setting in Maine was initiated in 1928 by the owners in collaboration with landscape architect Beatrix Farrand. Inspired by gardens that the owners had encountered on a trip to the Orient, and by the English-style border gardens they had often visited in Europe, they combined efforts to produce a spectacular garden that mixes elements from both East and West.

The Western influence can be seen in the central rectangle that makes up the informal annual garden and in the oval sun garden with its clear stone-embedded pool. Surrounding these is the Eastern-style portion of the garden anchored by a rosy-hued wall. Modeled on China's Forbidden City wall, it's crowned with that famous structure's coping stones, purchased when the original wall was being renovated. Outside this enclosure, with its lovely novelty-shaped gateways, is in all-encompassing perimeter of woodland featuring a stately display of Korean tomb figures, a Buddha, and other sculptural ornaments brought back from the Far East.

The solemn aspect of old Korean tomb figures that line the "Spirit Walk" beyond the main garden's enclosure wall.

Throughout the garden, pools are used to engender a feeling of tranquillity. OPPOSITE A rectangular reflecting pool captures the lovely tracery of leafy branches overhead. As part of a rigorous maintenance plan, the pool is emptied once a week and cleaned, so that when the wind is calm and the water still, the pattern of paving stones and the color details of the rocks can be seen through the crystal-clear water.

ABOVE Ancient looking flat rocks, scored by the elements over time, are arranged to form a primitive bridge spanning the water next to an antique stone ornament. LEFT In the moss garden, a primordial bench constructed from simple stone slabs creates the perfect spot for rest and reflection beside a rock pool.

OPPOSITE The figurative gateway is an important design element in Chinese garden architecture. When cut into a solid wall, the unusual shape draws the viewer's eye to the encapsulated scene beyond it, just as a frame captures the subject of a painting. This one, curved like a graceful urn, connects two halves of a garden path. ABOVE Another arresting example of the Eastern design influence in this garden is the circular-shaped Moon Gate. Because Chinese art reveres the principle of harmonious balance, including the counterpoise of sun and moon, the moon shape is also a cultural symbol that's often seen in its architecture. LEFT A massive gate folds back against the boundary wall whose coping incorporates remnants from the original Forbidden City wall. BELOW An arched gateway hewn from the boundary separating the central flower garden from the oriental sculpture garden.

CHOOSING STATUARY

Statuary, a gallery garden basic, doesn't have to be antique in order to be effective. The key, of course, lies in the quality of the piece itself—whether old or new. How to make the right choice? For those planning gallery gardens of their own, here are some tips on statuary to help get you started.

PLACING A CLASSICAL STATUE IN YOUR GARDEN
immediately establishes an atmosphere of antiquity—as if the garden itself dates back to the period represented by the statue. And this will hold true even if the garden is newly planted and the statue a modern reproduction.

WHEN CHOOSING A STATUE OF THE HUMAN FIGURE,
look for classical facial features and a pleasing expression. The body should be ideally proportioned. Original classic Roman statuary and pieces from Greece's later Hellenistic period often depicted very realistic human figures, warts and all, and sometimes you'll come across reproductions of these fascinating pieces. But whether you opt for real or ideal, the facial and body features should be realistic and detailed.

CLOTHING AND DRAPERY EFFECTS should also be carefully rendered. Study the folds in a section of fabric and, if the statue is clothed, the hang of that clothing. In the best pieces, you'll almost feel that if you reach out and touch it, your hands will meet the softness of cloth. And I particularly like statues with a sheer drapery effect that suggests the contours of the body beneath.

STATUES WITH PROPS (a male athlete with a discus, a female holding a book or vase of flowers) are always desirable because such handheld items add another element of interest to the figure itself.

ALL ELEMENTS SHOULD BE SHARPLY DETAILED
and etched deeply enough to withstand weathering without wearing down to an amorphous nothingness. The more refined the interpretation, the better the quality.

GALLERY ELEMENTS

Think of a gallery garden as a private exhibit where you, the curator, can display all the pieces you love living with and looking at. They might be museum quality or museum copies; fine one-of-a-kinds or a whole collection reflecting a single subject or style. In *this* gallery, the choice is all yours.

The Grecian-style urn and pedestal of white cast iron is a valuable antique, but quality reproductions of classics like this can be found in cast iron, or look-alike fiberglass.

A garden gate with elegantly simple design details that make it worthy of being called classic and, as such, an equally worthy addition to any gallery garden.

No gallery would be complete without a bench for viewing the exhibits at leisure. This splendid example of cast-iron art is a Victorian antique.

Sometimes you'll find a piece that was modeled after a museum antique. Such is the case with this artfully rustic settee of welded steel "twigs" copied from furniture in Delaware's Winterthur Museum.

A classical Gallic formality infuses this gravel-paved gallery room that's the display space for a collection of Victorian French wire chairs which the owner separately acquired over a period of years.

An antique garden armchair of basket weave cast iron is not only lovely to look at, but also surprisingly comfortable to sit in, a consideration to keep in mind when buying any chair or bench for your garden.

the whimsical garden

OF ALL THE THEMES in this book, the whimsical garden is one of my favorites, because it's all about humor and entertainment and serendipity. Like all garden designs, the whimsical style mimics interior-design principles to some degree, but it defies the usual constraints imposed by space or convention and blithely goes about turning those principles upside down. It's almost as if this is the way orthodox rules would behave if someone let them outdoors to play. That's not such a far-fetched metaphor, because there's a wonderful childlike quality to whimsical gardens that appeals to the playful sense in all of us.

Take color, for instance. Whereas vivid colors for indoor rooms have to be handled with care, the outdoor setting combined with the permissiveness of this garden style lets you lavish color as freely as you like. You can have fences, furniture, and a quaint little garden shed all brightly painted with colors straight out of a crayon box—neon lilac, brilliant yellow, or a shade of green that even nature couldn't come up with. Whenever you look at such colors, you can't help but feel instantly cheered. That's part of the charm: Whereas most gardens are meant to soothe the senses, the whimsical garden stimulates, amuses, and delights them.

Of course, color isn't the only way to create this effect. Another approach might be to furnish your outdoor space with elements borrowed from a classical interior. Imagine walking into a wooded clearing and finding a beautiful teakwood settee next to a table and a candelabra, all conventionally arranged on a thick carpet of leaf-strewn pine needles. You suddenly have the curious sensation that you have stumbled into a wood nymph's parlor, and a very tastefully furnished one at that. It's the total unexpectedness of seeing those indoor elements in an outdoor setting that makes you want to laugh aloud with delight. Or how about dining alfresco on a fabulous table that's supported by terrazzo stone balusters and bathed from above by the light of a hanging crystal chandelier? All the ornaments are perfectly conventional; the whimsy lies in the fact that they're used in such unconventional places.

Having fun with size and proportion is still another way of creating a sense of playful interest. How about furnishing your garden with a living room chair that happens to be three times the normal size? This isn't something you could get away with inside a house, but you can here. Whereas an outsized sculpture might overwhelm an interior space, it could feel right at home in this kind of outdoor space. So too would an enormous stone jar or, for that matter, several of them positioned at a narrow entrance point to the garden or at opposite ends of a closed path. The surprising juxtaposition of outrageously large objects against small or confined areas makes viewers stop short. When they do, they find themselves really noticing—and appreciating—these objects in ways they might never do with more traditionally sized ornaments. Given the wide-open space and the weight-bearing capabilities of solid ground, you might also consider paving your garden with extra-large stone tiles. As you'll see in one of the gardens featured in this chapter, the tracery effect of moss on the variegated, peach-hued tiles creates an outdoor version of a lovely old Persian carpet.

If you happen to be a collector (and if what you've collected is sturdy enough to be out-of-doors), the free-form character of a whimsical garden makes it the perfect place for displaying your treasures. These might be amusing, furniture-like metal sculptures. Or a collection of antique garden chairs from the '20s, '30s, and '40s with no two of them alike, which is just fine, because in this singular type of garden, mismatching is key.

Many world travelers are keen collectors of souvenirs gleaned from the places they've visited. If you're such a collector, you might consider displaying these mementos in the garden. Use your trove of rocks from around the world to decorate the face of an otherwise ordinary stucco wall. Arrange those big burnished enamel vases (or carved stone masks, or small antique statuaries—whatever) with other pieces to create arresting vignettes for visitors to discover in an unexpected corner.

You might want to put one of your favorite finds to a creative and unintended use, as did the owner of a small ornamental house, originally fashioned to display a statue of Buddha, who converted it into a charming light for the garden, or the artist who used the two halves of an old arched shutter to create a compelling garden entranceway.

If there's any one rule of thumb about decorating a whimsical garden, it's this: display only truly interesting objects that you love. They may be quirky, or bright, or fun house in feeling. They may be conventional furnishings used in a totally new way. But if seeing them always brings a smile of pleasure, you'll know your effort was successful.

playing
with color

Bob Dash is a painter who loves gardening, so it's not surprising that his artist's feel for color has spilled over to the ornamental furnishings in the garden he calls "Madoo."

Situated in Sagaponack, Long Island, the property is a seemingly endless series of spaces where a palette of playful colors is used not only for its own sake, but also to emphasize the different fun-shaped components of the painted pieces themselves.

Dash's sense of whimsy doesn't stop with color. There are magical walkways to explore (including one made from crosscut circles of tree branches), unexpected bits of statuary to discover, and a grove of trees—like stage props for a child's fantasy—that's guaranteed to set even the dullest imagination soaring to whimsical heights.

In the background here is an ornamental arrangement of twisted branches and greenery which forms a little island that verges the lawn. And taking center stage is a whimsical bench-cum-barrow whose separate components are emphasized by bright splashes of complementary color.

OPPOSITE Another Dash innovation is this cast-iron fountain with a circular base of spaced stones to channel the water into a little pool beneath. ABOVE, LEFT Metal chairs and a matching drinks table in eye-catching mustard yellow. ABOVE The typical Dash touch seen in a sculptural composition that might be titled "Big Basket with Standing Poles." LEFT Two earthenware jars of dried allium before a fenced-in topiary garden.

LEFT The octagonal shape of a dining table with matching stools is repeated in the contours of the sunny little gazebo in which the pieces are so snugly placed. BELOW, LEFT A broader view of the same structure showing one of its cleverly designed panels between two thriving cedars. BELOW No reason why whimsical can't be practical as well. Here, an amusing walkway is paved with the sliced cross sections of tree logs. OPPOSITE With its bright colors and decorative oval-shaped pipes, a pagoda-roofed footbridge also serves as a delightful platform for taking in the surrounding woodland landscape.

woodland fantasy

Eclecticism is a key ingredient in the whimsical style of ornamentation, and Diane Benson's garden in East Hampton, Long Island, has that quality to the nth degree. Combining her love of world travel and collecting with an equally fervent devotion to gardening, she's created a woodland fantasy that's filled with vases, urns, furniture (indoor as well as outdoor), sculpture, and delightful oddments that defy categorizing. It's a wonderful mix of East and West, ancient and abstract, serious and playful, and what's more, it all works like a dream.

ABOVE, LEFT Free-form metal cutouts function as slats for an imaginative border fence by artist Peter Jezvremov. LEFT In one cozy garden corner, a Guatemalan monkey table and stools invite visitors to relax with a cool drink. OPPOSITE A teak sofa from Indonesia is arranged with coffee table and candelabrum. The whimsy, of course, isn't in the traditional arrangement, but in its woodsy outdoor setting where, on warm evenings, Benson entertains guests by candlelight.

OPPOSITE One noteworthy example of the garden's collection of sculptures is this surrealist metal twig chair that was originally created by sculptor Robert Wilson as part of the stage set for a Broadway play. LEFT While the horse head with jars composition wouldn't seem out of place in a traditional living room, it also makes a nice vignette for the corner of a pool. Both the 19th-century jade head and the antique porcelain jars came from China. BELOW, LEFT Sometimes you come across "found sculpture": an unusually shaped piece of driftwood, a rare seashell, or, as shown here, a large hunk of striated stone bought by the owner from a local stone merchant. BELOW An arresting vision beside a garden fence is this stone hand which originally came from a ruined Buddhist statue in Thailand.

scenes from the past

A whimsical garden is the ideal place for indulging your fondest fantasies, as the owner of this property did when he fashioned his old-world garden in West Cornwall, Connecticut. Educated as a landscape architect, Michael Trapp has an additional talent for stage-set design. It becomes evident when you walk through his multileveled spaces and see the delightfully unexpected ways he's used his collection of classical architectural elements to create an atmosphere reminiscent of ancient Greece and Rome. Some of these objects are old; some are treated to look that way. And some—such as the crystal chandelier that cantilevers from a tree trunk—are out-and-out bits of fun to remind the visiting "tourist" that even classical ruins should never be taken too seriously.

ABOVE LEFT A sculptural antique urn ornaments a garden space near the house. LEFT Trapp's collection of cement balusters in temporary storage. OPPOSITE Typical of Trapp's ingenuity with architectural remnants is his vision of an Italian villa entry gate that he fabricated from two Ionic columns, vintage louvres, and a pair of asymmetrically planted pots.

OPPOSITE One of the best things about a whimsical garden, and this one especially, is that the playfulness of the pieces and settings don't slip quietly past the viewer's notice. A good illustration of that phenomenon is this narrow, walled-in path with a giant olive jar marking each of its corners. The size contrast of path and pots grabs the attention by force, inducing the same amused disorientation we find in a fun house.

ABOVE A garden terrace cobbled like an old European city street is a relaxing setting for a plant-bordered grouping of unmatched chairs.

RIGHT A classically modeled bust reposes within a seemingly casual arrangement of ivy tendrils and strewn rocks.

OPPOSITE Wherever the eye rests, there's always something wonderful to look at, including this antique stone birdbath posed in a woodsy tableau beside a baluster-railed terrace. ABOVE An antique cast-iron fountain on a graceful pedestal circled with swans. ABOVE, RIGHT Another example of classic elements put to inventive uses. The massive limestone paving tiles (from a Loire Valley chateau) create an elegant Persian carpet design for the dining terrace. Hanging above the baluster-legged table: the surprise of a crystal chandelier that cantilevers from the supporting trunk of an adjacent tree. RIGHT Square columns of weathered wood uphold the rustically classic arch of a stone-floor footbridge.

tropical
teasers

Novelist Brian Antoni divides his time between a residential hotel in Manhattan and his home in Florida's exuberant South Beach. Years ago, to create a buffer zone between his house and the area's "twenty-four-hour carnival" ambience and its excesses (ironically captured in his second book, *Eye of the Orgy*), he began planting a veritable jungle of greenery, which is now a backdrop for his own carnival of whimsical garden ornaments.

Because he loves pieces that are humorously surreal, the garden is filled with funny surprises, such as a footpath of cartoonish footprints or a "sculpture" that incorporates plastic spoons. Even better, Antoni loves embellishing serious pieces with his own puckish touches, such as a pair of statues representing Venus and Neptune: She's wearing false eyelashes and he's got a plastic lobster skewered on his trident. In other words, it's the kind of garden that whimsy is all about.

ABOVE, LEFT A takeoff on the 1950s-style driveway replaces the usual center swath of lawn with sprightly mondo grass. LEFT A (literal) footpath made from old cement molds. OPPOSITE Suggesting the quirky image of a diving mermaid is a gilded fish tail whose scales are plastic Baskin-Robbins spoon bowls! FOLLOWING PAGES, LEFT Bedizened figures of Venus and Neptune beside a grid-gated entry. RIGHT The Styrofoam mask is from The Institute, an old Miami nightclub. Antoni's contributions are feature-limning seashells and a palm-fronds headdress.

BUILDING A WALKWAY

A random pattern of tree trunk chunks set in a bed of sand and gravel serves as an attention grabber of a walkway. It was the invention of Bob Dash, who thought up the idea to enhance his garden. If you can saw logs, you can easily make this special walkway for your own garden.

BEFORE YOU START, read all the directions.
Also see page 200 for general wood-project guidelines.

FOR THIS PROJECT YOU'LL NEED:
- String line and wooden stakes
- One-by-eight pressure-treated lumber (CCA), length as needed
- Sand and/or gravel for filler
- A 3-foot length of two-by-four (for smoothing filler surface)
- Assorted-sized logs of oak, locust, or other hardwood, each measuring about 4 to 6 inches in diameter
- Hand saw or chainsaw
- Wooden mallet or hammer

STEP 1: Lay out the proposed area for your walkway by marking its perimeters with string lines tied to stakes.
STEP 2: Shovel topsoil from the whole marked area to make a flat-sided trench that's 8 inches deep.
STEP 3: Place the one-by-eight (CCA) boards against the flat sides of the entire perimeter to make a retaining wall/border.
STEP 4: Fill trench to a depth of 3 inches with hard-packed filler to make a solid bed for the log sections. Use the 3-foot piece of two-by-four to smooth the filler as you go.
STEP 5: Saw the hardwood logs horizontally into 4-inch lengths and stand them closely together on the bed of filler in any pattern you like.
STEP 6: Shovel more filler over the logs and use a broom to help sweep it into all the open spaces between the logs.
STEP 7: Spray lightly with a garden hose so that the filler settles, then repeat the filling/watering process until the walk is level and solid.

The weathered frame of a defunct rowboat abandons its traditional beach setting for a spot on a garden lawn where it becomes the delightful receptacle for a tub of flowers.

The playful eye-catcher on this front lawn is a colorful garden bed that's been carefully planted to look as if the flowers were spilling out from the overturned wooden bucket beside it.

A bit of drollery placed beside a garden gate. The statue is a fantastical creature (with young) that's somewhat reminiscent of Tenniel's drawing of the Frog Footman in *Alice's Adventures in Wonderland*.

This garden owner, a collector of old farm machinery, has turned a vintage tractor into a machine-age sculpture displayed in a garden of wildflowers.

The unexpected juxtaposition of a formal crystal chandelier within a picnic setting creates an element of surprise.

In a paradoxical ploy that seems both natural and unexpected, a semicircular portico roof is used as a display shelf for a colorful collection of urns and a statue representing the famous Botticelli painting sometimes irreverently referred to as "Venus on the Half-Shell."

WHIMSICAL ELEMENTS

Ornaments for a whimsical garden might be witty sculptures ranging from fabulous to folk. They can be garden-variety furnishings set up in clever ways or in unexpected places—or even "found" pieces borrowed from non-garden environments. But always, they should amuse and delight.

resource guide

WOOD-PROJECT GUIDELINES

Wood used for any outdoor project should be chosen with the environment in mind. Teak and Honduran mahogany are prime choices that, finished or unfinished, won't rot or weaken even after years of weathering. They are, however, very expensive. More economical choices are redwood, cedar, and white oak, which have respectable life spans, especially when stained with an oil-based preservative. Chemically treated wood, called CCA, can also be used outdoors.

WOOD MEASUREMENTS: "Two-by-two" is a lumber-yard term for lengths of wood that are actually $1\frac{1}{2}$ inches thick on all sides; a "two-by-one" really measures $1\frac{1}{2}$ inches wide by $\frac{3}{4}$ inch thick.

NAILS OR SCREWS used for any outdoor wooden structure should be rust-proof, so opt for those made of galvanized steel, stainless steel, or copper.

OIL-BASED STAINS are recommended for finishing and protecting wooden ornaments used for growing plants because, unlike paint, stains don't require sanding between coats. This means you can touch up the structure when needed without disturbing the plants that are growing on it. A good stain can be made by mixing equal parts of turpentine and any oil-based enamel.

Bathing figure

Kenneth Lynch & Sons, Inc.

A producer of ornamental products since 1930, Lynch specializes in beautifully detailed cast stone statues, but also offers some wonderful curbing, fountains, birdbaths, benches, weather vanes, sundials, and topiaries —all artistically crafted from a variety of materials, including cast stone, Ipe wood, lead, cast iron, steel, copper, and other metals.

P.O. Box 488
84 Danbury Road
Wilton, CT 06897-0488
(203) 762-8363

Catalogue available

"Summer" on pedestal

Urn with lead handles

"Hunter"

Figure with piped shell

Roundbush finial

LEFT: *Westbury urn without handles;* RIGHT: *English garland urn; Guggenheim bench*

Roundbush Castings, Ltd.

Roundbush is known for their intricately detailed fountains, planters, urns, and other accessories fashioned from a special fiberglass compound that amazingly mimics (and even weathers like) stone and lead.

Order through Exterior Decor (800) 355-6632

Chelsea urn with handles and Chelsea pedestal

Vau Le Vicomte fountain base and Timpidiom fountain top

Alligator birdbath

Square medallion planter

Nefertiti throne

Large basketweave planter

Large Florentine planter

Mecox Gardens

Mecox carries a range of unique garden furniture, plant stands, pots, and other accessories, including handsomely reproduced pieces based on one-of-a-kind museum models.

William McDowell Hoak
257 County Road, 39A
Southampton, NY 11968
(516) 287-5015

Mecox Gardens
962 Lexington Avenue
(at 70th Street)
New York, NY 10021
(212) 249-5301

Mecox cast cement pot

Mecox cast cement pot; large globe ivy topiary

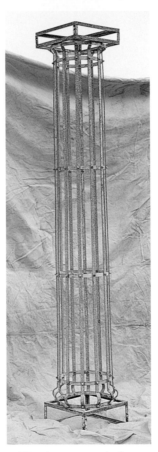

Mawson bench in teak by Munderskiles

*Mt. Vernon fruit tree box
in mahogany by Munderskiles*

Wrought-iron painted column

Wrought-iron armchair

Metal folding café table

*Mawson chair in teak
by Munderskiles*

*Ferrand tea table by Munderskiles
available in mahogany and teak;
cement sphere*

The Phillips Collection

A terrific source for unusual home and garden furnishings, Phillips specializes in quality ornaments of natural materials handmade in Sri Lanka, Indonesia, Turkey, and other ports of call around the world.

Order through
Exterior Decor
(800) 355-6632

Smithsonian Fern Leaf Collection

Brown Jordan

This particular collection offers cast aluminum garden furniture in a number of styles. If you're looking for clean lines and authentic design, Brown Jordan is the place to go.

Order through
Exterior Decor
(800) 355-6632

Stone Buddha head

Tree-leaf wrought-iron screen

Volcanic stone Buddha heads

Tulip design wrought-iron planter with removable container

Wooden wheel bench

Antique mercury balls for the garden

Howard/Linda Stein Antiques

These antique dealers specialize in unique pieces for the home and garden.

Order through
Exterior Decor
(800) 355-6632

Bayberry Nursery

In addition to plant materials, this delightful thirteen-acre nursery also features a select group of garden pieces, including teak furniture, lead, fiberglass, and wood planters, and stone and terra-cotta pottery, all with a distinctly European flavor.

50 Montauk Highway
Amagansett, NY 11930
(516) 267-3000

Soaring 12-foot stone obelisk

Limestone puzzle chairs

Antique stone wild boar

Wood dovecote

Kew fountain on pedestal

Teak table with surrounding benches

Stone and mahogany bench

Mexican-style limestone chair

Marble fountain from northern Italy, circa 1890

Nineteenth-century Romanesque lion of Verona marble

Carved brownstone and granite column, circa 1890

R. T. Facts

Owners Greg and Natalie Randall have gathered a wonderful selection of garden and architectural antiques in the classical style so often seen in fine European gardens.

Old Town Hall
22 South Main Street
Kent, CT 06757
(860) 927-1700

Cast stone Art Deco griffins

Antique terra-cotta boar made in England, circa 1890

Paradis Garden Arts

Their specialty is heavy-duty cast-iron and wood yard furniture and urns, including some lovely pieces with the black-green finish so typical of French garden antiques.

Order through
Exterior Decor
(800) 355-6632

Marble and cast-iron console table

Cast-iron and painted teak chairs and matching ottomans

Classic armchair

Stone finial and cast-iron urn

French-style park bench

Urban Archeology

Visiting UA is like discovering a museum of original and unique period ornaments for inside and outside that used to adorn city buildings, streets, and parks in the last century. The bonus—all of these exhibits are for sale.

143 Franklin Street
New York, NY 10013
(212) 431-4646

Also at:
Elizabeth Street Gardens
1176 Second Avenue
(at 63rd Street)
New York, NY 10021
(212) 644-6969

Redwood trellis fence and gate

Munderskiles

One of the enticements that makes midtown Manhattan such a shopper's paradise, Munderskiles carries fine quality copies of historic American garden furniture in teak, exquisitely rendered by designer John Danzer.

799 Madison Avenue,
3rd floor
New York, NY 10021
(212) 717-0150

The following is a list of affordable stores and catalogs with great-looking garden ornaments.

Pottery Barn

Specializing in home accessories, Pottery Barn also carries a nice line of French bistro chairs, patio furniture, and a good general selection of garden accessories.

(800) 922-5507

Crate & Barrel

A great home furnishings source that also carries a unique line of contemporary patio and outdoor-dining furniture.

(800) 451-8217

Home Depot

Though widely known as a home improvement supply source, their stores also feature a sizable garden department that includes a nice selection of furniture, urns, planters, and other garden accessories. Over 700 stores nationwide.

(800) 433-8211

Devonshire

Devoted strictly to garden ornaments, including some antiques as well as beautifully made new pieces.

Main Street
P.O. Box 1860
Bridgehampton,
NY 11932

Call for other locations:
(516) 537-2661

Smith & Hawken

Completely devoted to gardeners and gardens, Smith & Hawken can be relied on for tastefully designed teak, cast-iron, and aluminum furniture, as well as for lights, ornaments, and other useful accessories for outdoor decorating and entertaining. Catalog available.

(800) 776-3336

Gardener's Eden

A cornucopia of everything to do with garden ornaments, featuring different styles of pieces both functional and decorative.

P.O. Box 7307
San Francisco, CA
94120-7307
(800) 822-9600

Romancing the Woods, Inc.

If you love rustic style, you'll want to investigate this terrific source of rustic garden furniture, arbors, and primitive-looking accessories.

33 Raycliffe Drive
Woodstock, NY 12498
(914) 246-6976

Country Casual

This catalog company is a great source for English teakwood garden furniture and site furnishings.

9085 Comprint Court
Gaithersburg, MD 20760
(800) 284-8325

Walpole Woodworkers

These stores are a good place to go for traditionally styled cedar furniture, fencing, gates, and other garden accessories. For locations or a catalog, call (800) 343-6948.

FUNCTIONAL PRIMITIVE FURNITURE

In Devon, England, Paul Anderson fashions unique rustic garden ornaments that also function as furniture. Using recycled oak from ancient joists, weathered gates, and old fencing posts, Anderson's creations are inspired by the character of the wood itself—knots, nail holes, and all. For more information, write to him at 104 West Street, Hartland, Devon, England EX39; telephone 01237-441-645.

index

Page numbers in *italics* refer to illustrations.